AN INVITATION FROM RICK PERRY

With the nation in turmoil, why are our political leaders the most neglected mission field in America today?

I've wondered about this for quite some time. When I served as U.S. Secretary of Energy in Washington, D.C., nothing prepared me better for the work that needed to be done for our nation than the hour I spent every week in the Capitol Ministries White House Cabinet Bible Study. Our political leaders desperately need God's Word and yet they are all but forgotten when it comes to evangelism and discipleship. Let's fix that.

I'm teaming up with Capitol Ministries to reach public servants in city and county governments across America. Every week, these local servants will be reading the same studies that have been taught to U.S. national leaders in Washington, D.C. It's a daring vision but we already have the Bible studies written specifically to meet the faith needs, both personal and professional, of public servants. We are seeking men to teach them—retired businessmen, pastors, former pastors, lay leaders, and the person who senses his heart is being tugged by God.

Is this you? Capitol Ministries provides support, on-going training, and the Bible studies. As a local government ministry leader you will be joining a team that is committed to making disciples of Jesus Christ in the political arena throughout the world and sharing God's Word with the people whose very decisions impact our lives, help to create the society in which we live, and set the trajectory for our communities and our nation.

Visit capmin.org/local to learn more, and join me in sharing the Word of God with America's national leaders of tomorrow in your neighborhood today.

RICK PERRY
Former Secretary of the U.S. Department of Energy
Former Governor of Texas

UNITED STATES BIBLE STUDY SPONSORS

The following public servants sponsor the Capitol Ministries Bible studies led by Ralph Drollinger.

CURRENT AND FORMER GOVERNORS

Mike Dunleavy **ALASKA**
Greg Gianforte **MONTANA**
Sarah Huckabee Sanders **ARKANSAS**
Sonny Perdue **GEORGIA**
Rick Perry **TEXAS**
Jim Pillen **NEBRASKA**
Tate Reeves **MISSISSIPPI**
Kim Reynolds **IOWA**
Kevin Stitt **OKLAHOMA**
Scott Walker **WISCONSIN**
Glenn Youngkin **VIRGINIA**

SENATORS

Marsha Blackburn **TENNESSEE**
Mike Braun **INDIANA**
Katie Britt **ALABAMA**
Ted Budd **NORTH CAROLINA**
Bill Cassidy **LOUISIANA**
Kevin Cramer **NORTH DAKOTA**
Steven Daines **MONTANA**
Joni Ernst **IOWA**
William Hagerty **TENNESSEE**
Cindy Hyde-Smith **MISSISSIPPI**
James Lankford **OKLAHOMA**
Markwayne Mullin **OKLAHOMA**
Mike Rounds **SOUTH DAKOTA**
Tim Scott **SOUTH CAROLINA**
John Thune **SOUTH DAKOTA**

REPRESENTATIVES

Mark Alford MISSOURI
Robert Aderholt ALABAMA
Rick Allen GEORGIA
Don Bacon NEBRASKA
Michael Bost ILLINOIS
Josh Brecheen OKLAHOMA
Michael Conaway TEXAS
Rick Crawford ARKANSAS
Jake Ellzey TEXAS
Ron Estes KANSAS
Louie Gohmert TEXAS
Glenn Grothman WISCONSIN
Kevin Hern OKLAHOMA
Bill Huizenga MICHIGAN
Bill Johnson OHIO
Dusty Johnson SOUTH DAKOTA
Jim Jordan OHIO
Doug Lamborn COLORADO
Nathaniel Moran TEXAS
Kevin McCarthy CALIFORNIA
Gary Palmer ALABAMA
August Pfluger TEXAS
Bill Posey FLORIDA
Cathy McMorris Rodgers WASHINGTON
David Rouzer NORTH CAROLINA
John Rutherford FLORIDA
Glenn Thompson PENNSYLVANIA
Tim Walberg MICHIGAN
Randy Weber TEXAS
Daniel Webster FLORIDA
Bruce Westerman ARKANSAS
Brandon Williams NEW YORK
Roger Williams TEXAS
Joe Wilson SOUTH CAROLINA
Rob Wittman VIRGINIA
Steve Womack ARKANSAS
Rudy Yakym INDIANA
Ted Yoho FLORIDA

All in Authority

FOREWORD BY
SENATOR JAMES LANKFORD

All in Authority

*Reigniting the Bible's
Top-Down Missions Strategy*

Ralph Drollinger

CAPITOL
ministries®

All in Authority
Reigniting the Bible's Top Down Missions Strategy

Copyright © 2023 Ralph Drollinger

All rights reserved. No part of this book may be reproduced in any form or any means—electronic, mechanical, photocopying, scanning, or otherwise—without permission in writing from Capitol Ministries.

Published by Capitol Ministries, Santa Clarita, California, capmin.org

Unless otherwise indicated, all Scripture quotations are from the *New American Standard Bible*® (NASB®), Copyright © 1960, 1971, 1977, 1995, 2020 by The Lockman Foundation. Used by permission. All rights reserved. lockman.org.

Scriptures noted NKJV are taken from the *New King James Version*®. Copyright © 1982 by Thomas Nelson. Used by permission. All rights reserved.

Scriptures noted ESV are taken from *The Holy Bible, English Standard Version*. ESV Text Edition: 2016. Copyright © 2001 by Crossway Bibles, a publishing ministry of Good News Publishers. Used by permission. All rights reserved.

Scriptures noted NIV are taken from the *Holy Bible, New International Version*®, NIV® Copyright ©1973, 1978, 1984, 2011 by Biblica, Inc.® Used by permission. All rights reserved worldwide.

Part 1 of *All in Authority* is adapted and updated from the author's previous book, *Rebuilding America*, published by Nordskog Publishing, Inc., Ventura, California, 2016.

Editor: Deborah Mendenhall
Book design: Leslie Colgin

ISBN 979-8-9879718-1-9

Printed in the United States of America

DEDICATION

To Danielle, my faithful wife, who is not only my soul mate, but also my partner in ministry. You are such a wonderful and great blessing to me—and without you, neither Capitol Ministries nor *All in Authority* would ever have existed. All of Proverbs 31:10–31 befits you, and in a verse, ***"Many women do noble things, but you surpass them all"*** (v. 29, NIV).

CONTENTS

Acknowledgments xiii
Foreword xv

PART I – HOW TO TURN THE WHOLE "WORLD UPSIDE DOWN" 1
The Exemplary Example of Paul the Apostle 7
Paradigm Examples from the Old Testament 21
New Testament Models of This Paradigm 31
The Paradigm Continues in the End Times 37
The Power of Prayer-Propelled Evangelism 41
The National Benefits of This Missional Priority 45
Summary 53

PART II – THE PREEMINENCE OF EVANGELISM AND DISCIPLESHIP AND THE ANALYSIS OF THE EPOCH OF A BUNGLING CHURCH 57
The Social Implications of John the Baptist's Evangelism 63
1776: The Puritan Pulpit Shapes American Culture 71
1877: The Encroachment of Theological Liberalism 75
1920: The Fundamentalist Reaction 83
1950: The Birth of Neo-evangelicalism 89
1975: The Birth of the Religious Right 93
Summary 97

PART III – RIGHTEOUSNESS EXALTS A NATION 99
The Necessity of Righteousness 103
The Progenitor of Righteousness 107
Five Defining Characteristics of Righteousness 111
Summary 121

**PART IV – WHOM DOES GOD HOLD RESPONSIBLE
FOR THE DIRECTION OF A NATION?** 125
Haggai's Five Prophecies 131
A Profound Play on Words 137
Insights from Sodom and Gomorrah vs. Postexilic Judah 141
Summary 145

**PART V – WILBERFORCE: A MAN WHO
"TURNED THE WORLD UPSIDE DOWN"** 147
What Motivated William Wilberforce? 151
Who Was Wilberforce? 155
Coming to Faith in Jesus Christ 159
Wilberforce's Crisis of Faith 161
The Life of a Saved Politician 163
Wilberforce's "Two Great Objects" 165
The Importance of Evangelism and Discipleship
in Wilberforce's Life 169
Wilberforce's Thoughts on Moralism 173
Summary 177

Conclusion 181
Endnotes 183
About the Author 193

ACKNOWLEDGMENTS

I am indebted to my beloved wife, Danielle, whose encouragement, support, and dedication proved invaluable to the writing of this book.

A special thank you goes to Deb Mendenhall and Leslie Colgin who have worked tirelessly for many months on the manuscript and layout, respectively. They, along with Sara Bunn, Ronnie Gonzales, Hannah Watts, Mary Lou Yochim, and Misty Day serve as CapMin's administrative and creative team. I am grateful for their indefatigable work ethic and passion for our mission.

I am so thankful for the incomparable team of men the Lord has surrounded me with—the creative, resourceful, dedicated, and hard-working directors and ministry leaders who tirelessly toil to fulfill our mission.

Daily, I thank our Lord for providing the talented, skilled, and principled Board of Directors—men and women who faithfully seek God's leading and freely give their abundant skills, talents, resources, and energy as we chart this ministry's ambitious course.

My heartfelt appreciation for the support of the CapMin team is beyond words.

I was inspired to minister to political leaders while in Seminary. To that end, I am especially grateful to have benefited from the excellent teaching of Dr. Larry Pettegrew, one of my outstanding seminary professors who, in many ways, helped me develop my theological understanding and commitment to exegesis.

And finally, I am grateful for those Christian men who will read this book, understand its biblical moorings, and accept the audacious challenge to teach the Word of God to local political leaders across this great nation.

FOREWORD

Ralph and Danielle Drollinger have invested years of their ministry life in national and state Capitols in our country and around the world. I have the privilege of sponsoring and participating in the Senate Members Bible Study that Ralph leads in Washington, D.C., every week. I know firsthand their commitment to Scripture and their calling to provide leaders a strong foundation of biblical truth. They are skilled disciple makers fulfilling the essential task of challenging political leaders to think and grow biblically.

All in Authority: Reigniting the Bible's Top-Down Missions Strategy provides a carefully reasoned-from-Scripture basis for why the Church and its leaders should serve public servants. The book was written by someone who has decades of experience living the principles included in this book. By evangelizing and making disciples of political leaders, Church leaders are not only preparing souls for eternity but they are also helping people in God's institution of the State understand biblical truth as they make the daily decisions that affect our nation. When a political leader learns to think biblically, the city, state, and nation thrive under biblical principles.

When we remember that most of the Old Testament and at least a third of the pages of the New Testament were written to, by, or about political leaders, we are reminded that God's plan for reaching all people includes **kings and all who are in authority**. After years of work, careful study, and interaction with our nation's leading public servants, Ralph has authored an in-depth biblical blueprint of how the Church can effectively and efficiently love, teach, and reach local, state, and national political leaders for Christ.

Pastors, this is your challenge to boldly carry the truth in love into places of responsibility and to God's ministers for good (Romans 13:4). If your church is not intentionally and consistently serving the elected officials in your area, it is time to hear the call to love and serve *All in Authority*.

JAMES LANKFORD
United States Senator, Oklahoma

PART I

*HOW TO TURN THE WHOLE
"WORLD UPSIDE DOWN"*

PART I

The book of Acts records how a small band of men—the apostles—in very short order impacted the *whole world* during the first century in which they lived. As one Bible translation states in Acts 17:6, Jesus' followers *turned the world upside down!*[1] This small team of uneducated, common men were not elite leaders, so how did they orchestrate such a huge disruption in such a short period of time? How did they reach the world with the gospel so quickly?

Have you ever stopped to think about their accomplishment? How did Jesus' disciples, in a matter of several decades, manage to fulfill the Great Commission and change the world during the time in which they lived? They had no printing presses to produce large amounts of literature, no radio or television, no Internet or social media devices. So how were they able to saturate the world with the gospel—changing lives, changing culture, and eventually changing the Roman Empire?

Scripture provides the answer: not only did they fulfill the Great Commission one soul at a time through a ministry of geometric evangelism and discipleship, but they succeeded *by concentrating on and impacting a particular element of society.*

Notice 1 Timothy 2:1–4 in this light. This part of *All in Authority* will include a deep dive into this most important passage:

> *First of all, then, I urge that requests, prayers, intercession, and thanksgiving be made in behalf of all people, for kings and all who are in authority, so that we may lead a tranquil and quiet life in all godliness and dignity. This is good and acceptable in the sight of God our Savior, who wants all people to be saved and to come to the knowledge of the truth* (NASB).

In this passage the Apostle Paul is urging his disciple Timothy, who is now pastoring the Church in Ephesus, to pray evangelistically and evangelize (per v. 4) not just *all people,* but *specifically* **kings and all who are in authority.**

Verse 1 begins, ***First of all, then...*** or *parakalo proton* in the Greek. *Parakalo* is a compound word comprised of the preposition *para* and the verb *kaleo*. *Para* means "to come alongside" while *kaleo* means "to call." Used together in its first-person tense, *parakalo* is an emphatic verb that means "I call you alongside." The Apostle Paul then prioritizes what he had just said by including the word *proton*, which means *"first of all,"* to stress the priority of what he is about to say. Importantly, *proton* is used in the Greek language to signify first in importance versus first in sequence.

More literally, my paraphrase of these opening words would read: "Pastor at the Church of Ephesus, Timothy, let me say first *[in the sense of sequence]* what you need to do first *[in the sense of importance]*...."

Paul wanted Timothy to continue his past ministry emphasis of giving precedence to evangelism (undergirding evangelism with evangelistic praying) not only for ***all people*** in general, but importantly relative to the thesis of *All in Authority*: for ***kings and all who are in authority.***

> Concern for political leaders was not an afterthought in Paul's missional strategy to fulfill the Great Commission; rather, his burden was a top priority and passion that ran the length and course of Paul's life after his conversion.

Here, uncovered in chapter 2, is the underlying basis for the direction Paul took. *This main concern in his ministry was one of the most significant—if not the most significant—elements that vastly differentiated first-century Church missions strategy from the missions strategy of the modern-day Church.* This biblical top-down missions strategy explains, I believe, why the former was so much more impactful than the latter. Keep in mind that the first-century Church fulfilled the Great Commission and changed the world in their generation, whereas today's Church has not.

Why is reaching ***kings and all who are in authority*** so important? It goes without saying that political leaders are often the most influential people in a society. Not only do they possess enormous power, but capital cities are usually located near the center of the state or province; city hall buildings are in the center of the city. Political leaders and political capitol buildings represent the hubs of power, influence, communications, and transportation; they brim with influence that reaches into the countryside.

This top-down missions strategy of winning leaders for Christ, planting churches, and creating outposts for Christ in these centers of power makes sense for the practical reason of greater efficiency, effectiveness, and impact on a nation as a whole.

Chapter 1

The Exemplary Example of Paul the Apostle

Saul, the infamous tormentor of Christians, experienced a dramatic, life-changing conversion on the road to Damascus. An in-depth understanding of Paul's conversion clarifies why he instructs Timothy in 1 Timothy chapter 2 to make reaching political leaders a priority.

SAUL BECOMES PAUL AND IS GIVEN A MISSION

In chapter 9 of the book of Acts, Saul was blinded by Jesus, instructed to go into the city and wait. Jesus then sent His messenger Ananias to tell Saul what had happened to him and what he was to do. Acts 9:13–14 states that Ananias was initially afraid to go because Saul was a well-known persecutor of Christians:

But Ananias answered, "Lord, I have heard from many about this man, how much harm he did to Your saints at Jerusalem; and here he has authority from the chief priests to bind all who call on Your name."

In answer to Ananias' hesitation, in Acts 9:15 the Lord revealed the reason he must go:

But the Lord said to him [Ananias], *"Go, for he* [Saul] *is a chosen instrument of Mine, to bear My name before the Gentiles and kings and the sons of Israel."*

Shortly after his conversion, Saul was renamed Paul by God and given his mission.

> Specifically, and to the point of this book, Jesus articulated that Paul was to go and proclaim Christ as the way of salvation to two people groups[2]—*Jews* and *Gentiles*. But additionally, notice from this passage that Paul was also to reach the affinity sphere[3] of *kings*.

In terms of overall missions strategies today, the inclusion of *kings* and political leaders, who are described in other Scriptures as *all who are in authority* (1 Timothy 2:2), has been underemphasized and largely overlooked. However, such neglect is not the case in this passage. Paul did not take this instruction from the second member of the Trinity regarding mission strategy lightly—nor should today's believers. Paul would incorporate these three aspects of his calling into the general and specific focus of his ministry.

Many cities in the Roman Empire had not heard the gospel. How then did Paul decide where he would next travel? He must have deliberated about many factors along the way, but undoubtedly, one of his primary considerations was the presence of political leaders. According to Acts 9:15, such a priority would have been a matter of obedience to Jesus' commissioning. Indeed, both riveting and informative, following his Acts 9:15 calling, *Paul traveled almost exclusively to capital cities*—the cities of greatest influence!

What resulted in the long term was an enormous advance of the gospel and fulfillment of the Great Commission—nothing less than men ***who have turned the world upside down!***

Illustrating Paul's obedience to and sense of seriousness about his Acts 9:15 call, he journeyed to the following provincial capital cities of the Roman Empire, where in many, he started churches:

- Paphos (Acts 13:6) was the capital city of Cyprus.
- Perga (Acts 13:13) was the capital city of Pamphylia.
- Pisidian Antioch (Acts 13:14) was the capital city of Southern Galatia.
- Iconium (Acts 13:51) was the capital city of Lycaonia.
- Thessalonica (Acts 17:1) was the capital city of Macedonia.
- Athens (Acts 17:15) was the capital city of modern Greece.
- Corinth (Acts 18:1) was the capital city of Achaia.
- Ephesus (Acts 18:19) was the capital city of Proconsular Asia.
- Rome (Acts 19:21) was the Imperial Capital of the Roman Empire.

> On his three missionary journeys, Paul pinpointed, went to, and planted churches in cities where ***kings and all who are in authority*** lived!

As he traveled, he additionally ministered to *Jews* and *Gentiles* for sure, but the point I want to make is this: *he was called specifically as well to disciple kings.* He entrusted this same missionary emphasis to Timothy in 1 Timothy 2—and ostensibly the future Church—as his personal ministry was ending.

Jesus intends for His body of believers to carry out this same missional strategy, priority, and principle today.

THE GOVERNING AUTHORITIES CONVERTED IN ACTS

The primacy of winning governing leaders to Christ is vividly portrayed throughout the book of Acts in yet another way: of the thirteen individual conversions recorded by Luke in his narrative account of the inception of the Church, at least seven are politically related. The common thread among the following converts is found in 1 Timothy 2:2, ***all who are in authority.***

- The Ethiopian eunuch, who served as the treasurer of Candace, the Queen of Ethiopia, is converted (Acts 8:27).
- Cornelius the centurion, a Roman military leader of one hundred men, is converted (Acts 10:17).
- Blastus, the king's chamberlain, i.e., treasurer, is converted (Acts 12:20).
- Sergius Paulus, a Roman provincial governor, is converted (Acts 13:7).
- The Philippian jailer, a trusted governmental official, is converted (Acts 16:30–31).
- Dionysius, one of the Areopagite judges, is converted (Acts 17:34).
- Publius, the governor of Malta, is converted (Acts 28:7).

This insight into those on whom the early Church leaders focused, subsequently won to Christ, and then discipled is powerful evidence of their obedience to their calling and their priorities in ministry.

To further illustrate the missional emphasis of Paul on his three missionary journeys as recorded by Luke in the book of Acts, I have chosen to include at least one witnessing incident to a governing authority. Unfortunately, the political leader did not repent. In Acts 26, Paul worked in not only his personal testimony but the gospel message when he addressed the Roman ruler, King Agrippa.

The king's response is stated in verse 28 (NKJV): *"You almost persuade me to become a Christian."*

Neither a respecter of persons nor impartial, Paul pulls no punches, speaking with all due respect to this ruler, but plainly and directly. This additional account serves once again to indicate the consistency of God's ambassadors' reaching out to governing authorities throughout the book of Acts in order to proclaim His glory and the way of salvation.

LUKE AND MISSIONAL PRIORITIES

Whom is Luke writing to in the book of Acts? Like in his Gospel account, he is penning his tome to ***most excellent Theophilus*** (cf. Acts 1:1; Luke 1:3), addressing the recipient of the book with a title reserved for governors (cf. Acts 23:26; 24:3; 26:25). From his greeting, Luke is evidently inscribing this account to and for the purpose of persuading this particular government official to come to faith in Christ.

> In addition to illustrating Paul's obedience to his calling in Acts 9:15, the one to whom Luke is writing may explain

> why more than half of the individual
> conversions he includes in the book of
> Acts involve politically related people.

Luke's purposeful inclusion of all the other governmental authorities' coming to Christ could be to convey to Theophilus that his colleagues were coming to Christ (intimating Theophilus should also) and to illustrate the fulfillment of Paul's calling in Acts 9:15. Luke's recording serves both purposes.

Also worth noting is that of the 27 New Testament books and their total respective word count, Luke penned, in his two books alone, essentially one third of the words of and in the New Testament—*for the purpose of persuading one political leader to come to Christ!*

Ostensibly, Luke also grasped the God-given strategic priority of reaching political leaders for Christ.

PAUL GOES TO ROME

Paul's Acts 9:15 commission is the reason he so passionately desired to visit the Imperial Capital of Rome and, for that matter, why he wanted to travel as far as Spain. In Acts 23:11b the Lord personally communicates another directive to Paul:

> *"Take courage; for as you have solemnly witnessed to My cause at Jerusalem, so you must witness at Rome also."*

The apostle had longed to fellowship with the church in the world's most powerful city (Romans 1:10–12), but the Acts 23 passage serves to suggest he had at least one other compelling reason to make the voyage: to fulfill his clear calling by Christ to evangelize Caesar!

Further to this point, in Acts 27:23–24 an angel of God (in this case, a direct messenger from Jesus) conveys this message to Paul.

Soon after, in the midst of a terrible storm with his ship apparently about to sink, Paul evidenced this third personal communique from Jesus Himself as recorded in the book of Acts when he relates the following to his shipmates:

> *"For this very night an angel of the God to whom I belong and whom I serve stood before me, saying, 'Do not be afraid, Paul; you must stand before Caesar; and behold, God has granted you all those who are sailing with you.'"*

Given the message of this passage, neither Paul nor the other passengers had any reason to fret that the ship would sink due to the ferocity of the horrific storm upon them. Why? Because aboard the ship was divinely destined cargo—a man with a calling who was obeying the marching orders of the Savior Himself!

To paraphrase the words of Scripture, Paul was saying, "Relax, shipmates! Nothing can sink this vessel because I am aboard, and I have an appointment with the Emperor!" (There's no reason to buy trip insurance when you travel with a guy like this!)

> Paul had a divine unction—
> a providential mission to take the
> gospel to Caesar, and he knew that
> nothing could possibly stand in his way.

Handpicked by the Savior of the world Who was the Lord of the storm, Paul would fulfill his destiny.

The Scriptures do not record the exchange between Paul and Caesar, nor does history record that Caesar was saved as a result of Paul's mission and ensuing witnessing efforts. Evidently, however, others in the Imperial Capital were! During his Roman-imposed imprisonment, Paul penned a letter to the Church in Philippi. In his closing remarks, he said the following:

> *All the saints greet you, especially those of Caesar's household* (Philippians 4:22).

Though no evidence indicates that Caesar repented, Paul had nonetheless been used by God supernaturally in the Imperial Palace. Paul was a man governed by obedience to the vivid memory of his arresting conversion, sobering commission, and specific calling.

Are we as profoundly obedient as Paul was to reach *all who are in authority*? How are we manifesting Jesus' commission to reach all of the capitals and governing authorities at every level of government in every nation of the world?

PAUL GOES TO SPAIN

Given the formation, distillation, reiteration, and manifestation of Paul's deep-seated calling, is it not reasonable to assume his intention to visit Spain had something to do with pursuing political leaders? Most certainly! How is that?

He desired to visit Spain after he had visited Rome. This conclusion is observable from his earlier letter to the Church at Rome in Romans 15:23–24:

> *But now, with no further place for me in these regions, and since I have had for many years a longing to come to you whenever I go to Spain—for I hope to see you in passing, and to be helped on my way there by you, when I have first enjoyed your company for a while.*

Spain, a mineral-rich colony on the westernmost edge of the Empire, possessed a population of Jews and Gentiles who had yet to hear the gospel. But of first importance, Spain was to the Roman Empire what Palm Springs is currently to America. This upscale retirement community for the wealthy—the rich and famous, the powerful and influential—was a center for movers and shakers, as well as for the elite of Roman thought and culture.

Spain was home for some of the most famous retired political leaders of the ancient world. The Roman emperors Trajan and Hadrian had both been born in Spain and lived there. The orator Quintilian, the writer Martial, and the statesman Seneca all resided in Spain. Appropriately, as recorded by Clement of Rome (writing in AD 95, after the final penning of the New Testament), Paul eventually did reach Spain and gave his testimony before the rulers.

Isn't that testimony just so fitting for him? True to his calling, the apostle earnestly and thoroughly labored to impact all the political leaders of the known world with the gospel!

Lest you think I am reaching a bit when I state the above details, notice what Paul said in Romans 15:23 that further reveals his extremely dialed-in missional focus: *now, with no further place for me in these regions....* Certainly, other smaller communities located around the city of Rome had no church, so why did he come to that conclusion?

> Paul possessed an Acts 9:15 calling that had created a deep-seated conviction, a laser-like focus, and passion for the salvation of Rome's past and present political leaders.

This calling informs us as to why he gave such an emphatic mandate to Timothy near the end of his ministry in the first cited passage: 1 Timothy 2:1–4. The Apostle Paul was driven to reach leaders for Christ!

This underlying reason is why the apostles had such an astonishing impact on the first-century world with the life-transforming truths of salvation in Christ. This insight into their mission serves to explain their huge influence on a world dominated by "Greek philosophy." Indeed, a ragtag team known as *the apostles **turned the world upside down*** in the first century! If modern-day missions embraced a similar focus, would we have the same impact? I think so.

The fact that the apostles ***turned the world upside down*** is all the more astounding when you consider that these chosen men had little in the way of credentials; they weren't exactly Ivy League intellectuals, nor even the sharpest knives in the drawer. But those apparent shortcomings were more than offset by their disciplined adherence to reaching ***all who are in authority*** for Christ.

Most church scholars today agree that the apostles fulfilled the Great Commission in the first century. How else could they have accomplished that mission had it not been for this God-given strategy as is evidenced in Acts 9:15 and 1 Timothy 2:1–4?

God Himself will someday say to the apostles, *"Well done, good and faithful servant..."* (Matthew 25:23, NKJV).

May each of us possess a similar passion based on what God has set before us: encompassed by so great a cloud of witnesses might we receive the upward prize of our calling and obtain an imperishable crown! *Think about that!* All else wanes in comparison to fulfilling God's commands and pleasing Him! May we experience that same indescribable ecstasy by disciplining ourselves today to execute a similar missional priority and receive the ultimate reward. Amen!

THE GENESIS OF GOD'S MISSIONAL PRIORITIES

The consuming evangelistic fervor to herald the gospel to ***kings and all who are in authority*** that encompassed Paul's life after his conversion is not exclusively enshrined with him. Expansively, this focus runs throughout the pages of Holy Writ from Genesis to Revelation; this missional priority is near to the heart of God.

Organizationally speaking, having established this missional priority via the life of Paul, additional abundant passages evidence this important principle: reaching political leaders for God is a missional priority replete throughout Scripture from Genesis to Revelation!

Israel was meant to be a beacon of God's glory—to shine forth His goodness and salvation into all the Gentile nations. More specifically, in order to accomplish this directive, she was called on *by* God to testify *of* God to the political leaders in all Gentile nations. The psalmist best personifies Israel's priority of outward, missional purpose in Psalm 119:46, which says:

I will also speak of Your testimonies before kings and shall not be ashamed.

The following passages serve to further build the case that evangelizing and discipling political leaders for Christ today has always been near and dear to God's heart—as is evidenced in and by the Old Testament.

In the book of Genesis, God promised Abraham that one day he would receive land, have numerous descendants, and be blessed (Genesis 12:1–3). Four centuries passed as Abraham's descendants expanded from one family to twelve tribes and then finally blossomed into a nation—the nation Israel.

Why did the Lord call Abraham and his descendants out of the world? Exodus 19:5–6 states that Israel was to be *"My own possession among all the peoples..."* (cf. Deuteronomy 4:20). In terms of missional purpose, Israel was called on by God to be His special people—the envoys of Yahweh—in order to proclaim the excellencies of God to all the other nations of the world.

> In a general sense, God intended for His people to become a light to the Gentile nations, and in a more specific sense, He expected His people to be a light to the leaders of those nations!

Regarding that *general* sense of calling, God says through the prophet Isaiah to the nation of Israel in Isaiah 60:3, *"Nations will come to your light...."* And simultaneously in a *specific* calling to political leaders, God says through the prophet Isaiah to Israel in the second part of the verse: *"And kings to the brightness of your rising."*

The construction of this passage from *general* to *specific* parallels that of 1 Timothy 2:1–4 (the specific Greek construction will be developed later in the book): *Prayers ... be made on behalf of all people* [general], *for kings and all who are in authority* [specific]....

This simultaneous *general* and *specific* construct occurs as well in Paul's calling in Acts 9:15:

> *But the Lord said to him, "Go, for he is a chosen instrument of Mine, to bear My name before the Gentiles* [general] *and kings* [specific] *and the sons of Israel"* [general].

Furthermore, in this regard, note Isaiah 49:6–7 in which the prophet Isaiah uses the same type of general-to-specific construction regarding Israel's engaging in outreach to the Gentile nations and their leaders:

> *He says, "It is too small a thing that You should be My Servant*
> *To raise up the tribes of Jacob and to restore the preserved ones*
>   *of Israel;*
> *I will also make You a light of the nations*
> *So that My salvation may reach to the end of the earth."*

Thus says the LORD, the Redeemer of Israel and its Holy One,
To the despised One,
To the One abhorred by the nation,
To the Servant of rulers,
"Kings will see and arise,
Princes will also bow down,
Because of the LORD who is faithful, the Holy One of Israel who
*   has chosen You."*

Isaiah 62:1–2 further evidences this same manner of outreach thinking:

For Zion's sake I will not keep silent,
And for Jerusalem's sake I will not keep quiet,
Until her righteousness goes forth like brightness,
And her salvation like a torch that is burning.
The nations will see your righteousness,
And all kings your glory;
And you will be called by a new name
Which the mouth of the LORD will designate.

The repeated simultaneous general-to-specific outreach calling of these passages could be summarized in the following way: *within the Great Commission exists the specific missional priority of reaching political leaders for Christ.* And I would go so far as to say that fulfilling this priority is the key not only to fulfilling the Great Commission, but also to advancing a nation.

The following chapters further illustrate this Old Testament principle—this missional priority God intended for Israel to carry out.

Chapter 2

Paradigm Examples from the Old Testament

The Old Testament brims with many accounts of God's ambassadors witnessing to kings and calling governing authorities to repentance. This part of *All in Authority* is not intended to be an exhaustive, comprehensive treatment of each of these occurrences, but rather an effort to further illume and cast a vision for this often-overlooked missional priority that is replete in the Old Testament. Note the sheer volume of Scripture that depicts God's called-out ones influencing kings. The relatively large number of references makes a statement in and of itself.

SOLOMON'S PRAYER OF DEDICATION

The significance of God's Old Covenant saints laboring to evangelize Gentile politicians is reflected in Solomon's prayer of dedication to commence and inaugurate the completion of the Temple. During his prayer, when Israel's King Solomon gave thanks to God (as recorded in 1 Kings 8:60), he reminded Israel that the Lord had blessed their nation in order to achieve an outward, general purpose:

So that all the peoples of the earth may know that the LORD is God; there is no one else.

But more specifically, Solomon-the-architect had designed the Temple with God's guidance to include an exceptionally large courtyard wherein the Gentiles were to come in and worship God—all in keeping with the purpose of proclaiming God's glory to the other nations of the world.

> As the nations witnessed the radiant light of Israel, the hope was that they would come from afar, led by their kings, to worship the God of Israel.

Isaiah 60:11 evidences this idea:

"Your gates will be open continually;
They will not be closed day or night,
So that men may bring to you the wealth of the nations,
With their kings led in procession."

God's desire in this Scripture is plainly seen: Israel was to be about heralding Yahweh's glory to the other nations (in general) and reaching their political leaders (in specific). This desire was the holy purpose for including the Temple courtyard in the overall design, and it explains why Jesus, the ultimate architect of the plaza, would one day cleanse it from its detestable misuse on two separate occasions (See John 2:14–16 and Mark 11:15).

Israel was to emphasize reaching political leaders for God as an integral part of her overall purpose. Unfortunately, due to her disobedience, Israel largely failed in this ministry to win the foreign nations and their leaders. Instead of setting a shining example for the pagan nations, Israel's behavior, for the most part, was no better than theirs. As a result, the pagan nations, for the most part, were duly unimpressed with God's people.

When Israel did follow God's commandments, pagan nations and their rulers took notice. The Old Testament records several instances where kings came to ***the brightness of*** [Israel's] ***rising.*** The following three examples serve to illumine three of those occasions.

THE QUEEN OF SHEBA

First Kings 10:1–9 records the Queen of Sheba's visit to Jerusalem during the reign of King Solomon. The queen had traveled a distance of 1,400 miles in a quest to satisfy her curiosity regarding all she had heard about ancient Jerusalem. At that time in the world, Jerusalem was outstanding—a mesmeric city in her bright splendor.

The nation must have been extremely alluring because I cannot imagine any lady's being willing to embark on what would amount to a 2,800-mile round trip atop a camel—from the location of modern-day Yemen—through a morass of endless, hot, desert terrain! Scripture indicates, however, that the trip must have been worth it all as apparently she did not leave disappointed:

> *Now when the queen of Sheba heard about the fame of Solomon concerning the name of the* Lord, *she came to test him with difficult questions. So she came to Jerusalem with a very large retinue, with camels carrying spices and very much gold and precious stones. When she came to Solomon, she spoke with him about all that was in her heart. Solomon answered all*

her questions; nothing was hidden from the king which he did not explain to her. When the queen of Sheba perceived all the wisdom of Solomon, the house that he had built, the food of his table, the seating of his servants, the attendance of his waiters and their attire, his cupbearers, and his stairway by which he went up to the house of the LORD, *there was no more spirit in her. Then she said to the king, "It was a true report which I heard in my own land about your words and your wisdom. Nevertheless I did not believe the reports, until I came and my eyes had seen it. And behold, the half was not told me. You exceed in wisdom and prosperity the report which I heard. How blessed are your men, how blessed are these your servants who stand before you continually and hear your wisdom. Blessed be the* LORD *your God who delighted in you to set you on the throne of Israel; because the* LORD *loved Israel forever, therefore He made you king, to do justice and righteousness."*

Luke 11:31 provides the conclusion to this wonderful story.

"The Queen of the South will rise up with the men of this generation at the judgment and condemn them, because she came from the ends of the earth to hear the wisdom of Solomon; and behold, something greater than Solomon is here."

During her visit, or perhaps as a result of her visit, she was converted! Israel's corporate testimony (at that time) proved quite compelling—the nation was in touch with God's script as to how best to evangelize foreign Gentile leaders!

THE BABYLONIAN RULERS

The second example of Israel's overwhelming national charisma and fulfillment of her missional priority as a nation is found after the reign of Solomon during the reign of King Hezekiah. At some point in Hezekiah's rule, political leaders from Babylon were enamored enough to pay a visit to Jerusalem. States 2 Chronicles 32:31:

> *Even in the matter of the envoys of the rulers of Babylon, who sent to him to inquire of the wonder that had happened in the land....*

Hezekiah too followed God's script, and the astonishment of Israel served to evoke the interest of the Babylonians to pay a special visit; whether they were converted remains unknown.

Unfortunately, those two visits by Gentile political leaders are the only corporate illustrations in the Bible of Israel's fulfilling her external calling. What follow, however, are perhaps the most powerful biblically recorded encounters between one of God's prophets and a Gentile king relative to illustrating the association between the proclamation of the good news of salvation and the impact that such a proclamation has on the sociological and cultural direction of a nation.

THE PROPHET JONAH

The final Old Testament illustration I have chosen to elaborate on that serves to underscore Israel's embracing her missional mandate is the ministry of the Jewish prophet Jonah. Though a reluctant minister, Jonah eventually (after one whale of a roundabout journey!) reported to his assignment. He eventually resolved to obey God's call and proclaim His glory to the Gentile nation of Assyria in general and, more specifically, to the king of that nation and the capital city.

Of all the debauched countries in ancient history, ancient Assyria was perhaps the leader, a sewer of sin, and the worst depravity was flaunted in its capital city of Nineveh. For example, after Assyria conquered another nation, the conquered king would customarily be skinned alive in the Nineveh public square.

The book of Isaiah documents the Assyrians' history of intimidating the nation of Israel. Certainly, Jonah felt he had good reasons to despise his prophetic assignment. The idea of preaching to that arrogant country with its despicable practices must have seemed not only emotionally undesirable, but foolhardy and virtually impossible.

I can hear Jonah declaring, "What, God?! They will never repent!"

But to his amazement, the book bearing his name records that the nation in general did listen to his preaching, and soon Jonah had a specific audience with the king. Now himself transformed from being sidelined inside a big fish three days and nights by God for his disobedience, he is filled with courage, boldly calling the political leader to faith in Yahweh.

What followed provides an insight for those interested in impacting their nation for good in the here and now. *Just as nations fall from within, they are turned around from within! Not only did the king listen, but he ordered the entire nation of Nineveh to repent along with him!* Jonah 3:3–9 states,

> *So Jonah arose and went to Nineveh according to the word of the* Lord. *Now Nineveh was an exceedingly great city, a three days' walk. Then Jonah began to go through the city one day's walk; and he cried out and said, "Yet forty days and Nineveh will be overthrown."*

> *Then the people of Nineveh believed in God; and they called a fast and put on sackcloth from the greatest to the least of them. When the word reached the king of Nineveh, he arose from his throne, laid aside his robe from him, covered himself with sackcloth and sat on the ashes. He issued a proclamation and it said, "In Nineveh by the decree of the king and his nobles: Do not let man, beast, herd, or flock taste a thing. Do not let them eat*

or drink water. But both man and beast must be covered with sackcloth; and let men call on God earnestly that each may turn from his wicked way and from the violence which is in his hands. Who knows, God may turn and relent and withdraw His burning anger so that we will not perish."

What a fascinating piece of history! What a compelling illustration of the results that are possible from obeying God's missional priority!

> Like Jonah of old, when the Church today emphasizes the priority of reaching political leaders within the Great Commission, it is possible, too, that a whole nation can be turned to God both efficiently and effectively!

At least to some degree, Old Testament Israel understood God's missional mandate as represented by these four previous insights: the design and inaugural prayer over the Temple courtyard, the visit of the Queen of Sheba, the visit of the Babylonian rulers, and the missionary journey of Jonah to a Gentile nation and its leader. All serve to illustrate that Israel understood (and at times embraced) the profound calling of God to proclaim His love and salvation to the political leaders of the world.

May that be the case today in the Church Age!

ADDITIONAL OLD TESTAMENT EXAMPLES

God's Old Testament saints served as types and shadows of what New Testament believers were to embrace wholeheartedly. Examples of those God used to evangelize Gentile leaders are sprinkled throughout the books of the Old Testament as examples for today's Christians.

JOSEPH AND PHARAOH

In Genesis chapter 41, the Egyptian Pharaoh asks Joseph to interpret his dreams. In the course of doing so, Joseph boldly states twice: ***God has told to Pharaoh what He is about to do*** (v. 25b) ***and God will quickly bring it about*** (v. 32b).

The Hebrew word for "God" which Joseph declares to Pharaoh is not the same name used by Pharaoh to describe his pagan god. Joseph uses ***Elohim***, the formal name of the God of his great-grandfather, Abraham, to describe the one true God. Importantly, Joseph courageously insults Pharaoh's pagan god in the preamble of his interpretation!

> Interestingly in this narrative passage, Pharaoh acknowledges Elohim with his own responsive word choice in Genesis 41:39!

Pharaoh then prudently and wisely appointed Joseph to administer his empire. It would be a stretch, I think, to suggest that Pharaoh's choice of words represents an eternally successful proselytizing encounter. Nonetheless, Pharaoh's empire is profoundly influenced for good (Genesis 41:57) due to the ministry of Joseph in the life of a king.

Accordingly, this account serves to underscore and illustrate the analogy of Scripture, i.e., parallel passages in the Bible that declare the same principle. In this regard, note what Solomon states in Proverbs 14:34: ***Righteousness exalts a nation....***

God's appointed representative who proved faithful, persevering, and diligent to minister to a pagan king resulted in a more prosperous nation for all! Not only is this account illustrative of Proverbs 14:34, but the passage also serves to specifically and directly manifest the principle found in 1 Timothy 2:2b. This already addressed passage states the why of witnessing to *kings and all who are in authority*. Why should believers evangelize political leaders? The Apostle Paul provides the answer: *so that we may lead a tranquil and quiet life in all godliness and dignity*. Again, this promise from God's Word in the New Testament is for the "here and now." Joseph's bold witness to Pharoah resulted in national blessing.

MOSES AND PHARAOH

In Exodus 4, God commissioned Moses to return to Egypt and stand before Pharaoh as His spokesman. Through the next ten chapters, Moses witnesses to Pharaoh regarding God's power, greatness, and ability to deliver. God's servant is empowered and emboldened.

Unfortunately for Pharaoh and Egypt, Pharaoh is patently intransigent and unrepentant. Nonetheless, God uses Moses to impact the future of Egypt (Pharoah is about to lose his laborers), as well as the budding nation, Israel, via their deliverance from an oppressive ruler.

> Both Joseph's and Moses' separate accounts serve to illustrate how nations are immediately and powerfully impacted for good through the faithfulness of God's people interacting with *all who are in authority* (cf. Exodus 9:16; Romans 9:17).

SAMUEL AND KING SAUL

King Saul was Israel's first king, but he was not an obedient one. In 1 Samuel 13:13, God's ambassador Samuel confronts the nation of Israel's civil leader and boldly informs him of his need to repent from his sinful ways. God used His prophet Samuel, who was willing to confront Israel's first national leader.

This confrontation is quite similar to Paul's confronting King Agrippa. Neither King Saul nor King Agrippa repent. But both accounts nonetheless serve to underscore the point of this book: it is biblically normative for God's called-out ones to be witnessing to political leaders!

MORDECAI AND KING XERXES

Fast forward in the Old Testament to Israel in exile. Mordecai has become the second-in-command as he serves over the entire Persian Empire under the Gentile King Ahasuerus (Xerxes). Similar to Joseph, by God's design, the king was attracted to Mordecai's proven, godly character. Though no evidence of Xerxes' conversion is recorded, this account in the book of Esther (see 8:2) serves to illustrate how ordinary people who are God's ambassadors are emboldened and elevated by Him to witness His greatness to political authorities and to achieve His purposes through them.

DANIEL AND KING NEBUCHADNEZZAR

In the book that bears his name, Daniel serves as God's man to the Gentile Kings Nebuchadnezzar, Belshazzar, and Darius. Suffice to mention here within the whole of this glorious account of the life of the prophet, he led King Nebuchadnezzar to faith in God per Daniel 4:34–37.

Chapter 3

New Testament Models of This Paradigm

The life of Paul and the history of Old Testament Israel provide evidence of God's emphasis on reaching governing authorities with His plan of salvation. Time and time again, God's ambassadors have heralded God's truth to those in charge of nations. Moving forward from the Old Testament, tracing this biblical thread through other epochs of the Bible is fascinating.

With that foundation in mind, allow me to work forward from Israel to the time of Christ in this chapter, visiting the apostolic period once again, illustrating the principle of missional priority via Peter, and then journeying into the future, i.e., the coming Tribulation period and the millennial kingdom period.

JOHN THE BAPTIST AND KING HEROD

Prior to the start of the Church Age (which begins on the Day of Pentecost; see Acts 2), John the Baptist boldly confronts King Herod about his sin in Mark 6:18. Mark 6:20 implies that this secular king found both the character and message of the Baptist appealing. Nonetheless, he eventually bowed to pressure and ordered John beheaded.

Again, depicted here is a faithful servant's willingness at any cost to obediently represent the ways of God to a civil leader with an eye toward the destiny of his soul more than the correction of his policies.

Even though it would take another 300 years, this was the day the Roman Empire began to be transformed by the coming power of the gospel in the Church Age!

JESUS AND HIS DISCIPLES

When Jesus first commissioned His twelve disciples—even before Saul's conversion in Acts 9—He told them something remarkably interesting in light of the thesis of this book. In Matthew 10:18, Jesus tells His disciples:

> *"And you will even be brought before governors and kings for My sake, as a testimony to them and to the Gentiles."*

This passage from the Gospels serves to reveal that He expected His earlier trainees to reach out to political leaders as well. The New Testament importance of reaching political leaders for Christ does not start with Paul in Acts 9; it begins with the disciples in Matthew 10!

Some might argue that being *"brought before governors and kings"* is a reference to the persecution many of them would suffer, but it is undeniable that many of them did reach out to those in authority. They willingly gave witness to political leaders about salvation in

Jesus. Matthew 10 is the first chronological recording of Jesus' commissioning and sending out His disciples. And so, in a precursor to Paul's instructions in 1 Timothy 2:1–2:

> Jesus states here what is first and most important. Reach not only the masses in general, but the political leaders too—most specifically.

Of great significance is the missional priority of reaching political leaders with the Word of God, which extends from the Old Testament nation Israel through to the beginning of the Church Age as is foreshadowed here with the disciples in Matthew 10 (even though this book began with the Apostle Paul in Acts 9, which is chronologically speaking, after this Gospel account).

The New Testament contains other ensuing illustrations of this missional priority in the Church Age.

THE APOSTLE PETER

One of the disciples commissioned by Jesus in Matthew chapter 10 later elaborates more fully on the principle that Jesus bestowed on him, that He also bestowed on others, and that He would eventually bestow on Paul.

The Apostle Peter also possessed that Jesus-embedded aspiration—the missional priority to reach those in authority—albeit Peter's heart to get the gospel to leaders is not as easy to ascertain from the Bible as are the other examples cited.

Carefully note that the context of 1 Peter 2:13–14, which is revealed in verse 12, strongly evidences his passion and zeal for bringing the message of salvation to the Roman leaders. What follows are these two Scriptures listed in reverse order (so as to make the connection more readily obvious):

> *Submit yourselves for the Lord's sake to every human institution, whether to a king as the one in authority, or to governors as sent by him for the punishment of evildoers and the praise of those who do right* (vv. 13–14).

Those who implement the intent of these verses will …

> *Keep your behavior excellent among the Gentiles, so that in the thing in which they slander you as evildoers, they may because of your good deeds, as they observe them, glorify God in the day of visitation* (v. 12).

In 1 Peter 2:12 the apostle is exhorting his "Jewish converts to Christ" audience to live exemplary lives among the Gentile *king…or to governors* for a specific purpose: that they may, as a result, *glorify God in the day of visitation.* This final clause is Peter's way of saying that he desires that they be saved! Peter's desire for Gentiles and Gentile-governing authorities throughout the pagan Roman Empire to come to know Christ is evidenced in 1 Peter 2:13–14.

This passage adds a great additional insight to the thesis of this book:

> The Apostle Peter explains the means by which political leaders best end up *glorifying God in the day of visitation*: by believers, i.e., those witnessing to them—submitting to the laws of the same civil authorities!

In essence, Peter is saying that poor conduct in the Church will equate to a poor testimony in the community and especially to the political authorities. Bad conduct, which includes ignoring or breaking the laws of the land as evidenced by lack of submission to governing authorities, would stand in the way of others' coming to faith in Christ. The overall context and meaning of this insightful passage underscores the premise of *All in Authority*.

Simply stated, evangelism to Gentile **governors and kings** will prove effective only if believers humbly submit to the laws they enacted (provided, of course, that these laws do not conflict with God's laws). In other words, if we want to provide a strong witness to political leaders, we must **keep** [our] **behavior excellent** and do **good deeds** while submitting to them. By obeying the laws of the land, believers **keep** [their] **behavior excellent**, which is key to maintaining a strong testimony.

Not only is 1 Peter chapter 2 an echo to Jesus' call to His disciples in Matthew chapter 10 and to the Apostle Paul's commissioning and his manifest response of obedience to be a witness to political leaders in Acts chapter 9, but the passage also instructs *how* to be a witness to political leaders! This passage explains how a follower *of* Christ most effectively reaches political leaders *for* Christ! If we expect to gain their audience, we must be careful to submit to their authority with this important caveat—providing that what they demand is biblical.

Now we will turn to the biblical epoch following the Church Age to again illustrate the point of this book.

Chapter 4

The Paradigm Continues in the End Times

The missional priority of reaching all in authority continues during this future epoch of great upheaval (as recorded in Daniel, 2 Timothy 4, and the book of Revelation).

THE TRIBULATION PERIOD

During the Olivet Discourse in Mark 13:7–9, Jesus taught on events that will unfold during the coming Tribulation period. Wars will erupt, natural disasters will occur, and persecution will be common for all of Christ's followers who come to Him during that seven-year period.

> *"When you hear of wars and rumors of wars, do not be frightened; those things must take place; but that is not yet the end.*

For nation will rise up against nation, and kingdom against kingdom; there will be earthquakes in various places; there will also be famines. These things are merely the beginning of birth pangs. But be on your guard; for they will deliver you to the courts, and you will be flogged in the synagogues, and you will stand before governors and kings for My sake, as a testimony to them."

Among the limited details Jesus provides regarding the coming Tribulation period is, interestingly, special mention of testifying to political leaders. In a parallel to His commissioning of the twelve in Matthew chapter 10, Jesus states in Mark chapter 13 that believers *"will stand before governors and kings for My sake, as a testimony to them."*

Within the Great Commission exists the repeated priority and need to reach political leaders for Christ—even during perilous times. Take note that this timeless principle runs throughout all the periods of the Bible! This missional priority is mentioned time and time again!

THE MILLENNIAL KINGDOM PERIOD

I am often amazed by the contempt that some believers nowadays show toward political leaders. An attitude of disrespect is understandable when office holders continually conduct themselves in ways that are unconstitutional and/or less than biblical. However, such attitudes run contrary to the respect *for the office* that is commanded of believers in 1 Peter chapter 2 and Romans chapter 13. While I am shocked by some Christians' disrespect for the office, I must confess that when I see a surfeit of scorn and gossip, there is an element I find a bit ironic. Let me explain. Believers need to respect and learn from political leaders today because tomorrow every believer will become one!

Subsequent to Christ's return, God's people will no longer minister to kings. According to 2 Timothy 2:12; Revelation 5:10, 20:4, and 20:6, the believers will *become* kings themselves! These passages, which are listed respectively, contain a recurring word: *"reign."*

If we endure, we will also reign with Him; if we deny Him, He also will deny us (2 Timothy 2:12).

"You have made them to be a kingdom and priests to our God; and they will reign upon the earth" (Revelation 5:10).

Then I saw thrones, and they sat on them, and judgment was given to them. And I saw the souls of those who had been beheaded because of their testimony of Jesus and because of the word of God, and those who had not worshiped the beast or his image, and had not received the mark on their forehead and on their hand; and they came to life and reigned with Christ for a thousand years (Revelation 20:4).

Blessed and holy is the one who has a part in the first resurrection; over these the second death has no power, but they will be priests of God and of Christ and will reign with Him for a thousand years (Revelation 20:6).

In the coming thousand-year millennial kingdom, those who have been previously redeemed by Christ will be given the privilege to rule with Him, under Him, on earth. When Christ returns and His kingdom has come, He will grant believers the governing positions similar to those who *now* hold them—but unlike kings and rulers of today who are subject to the Fall and sin, Jesus will be the ultimate, perfect civil ruler over all the earth. Believers will then reign sinless in their glorified bodies under His impeccable civil headship.

The English verb *reign*, which comes from the Greek verb *basilius*, is found in each of the foregoing passages. This Greek verb stems from the same Greek noun from which the English word "king" is derived. But even though the verb and noun are quite similar in the Greek, we do not say in English that "kings (noun) king (verb)." Rather, we say, "kings reign," and thus English Bible translators translate the Greek verb in that way. A gardener may garden, a painter may paint, and a driver may drive, but kings do not "king" in English. Therefore, when the previously mentioned passages repeatedly state that believers will someday king (reign) with Him, the implication is that we too will be governing authorities of sorts under His perfect rule and authority.

If you are a believer reading this book, get ready to "king" in your future life! These passages indicate that such a position in society is your destiny! So if for no other reason than respect for the office of an institution God has ordained, put away those bad attitudes you might possess regarding those in this God-ordained institution. Someday you too will be a part of this institution when Christ returns and you reign under Him in His kingdom!

Believers will someday (soon I hope) become the consummate, perfect governing authorities! Praise God!

In the future, the type of ministry every believer will possess toward governing authorities will radically change—from one of *pursuing* governing authorities *for* Christ to one of *being* a governing authority *with* Christ.

These future-period passages serve once again to illuminate God's keen interest in governmental leaders throughout the whole of Scripture! His interest in political leaders remains intact even during the millennial kingdom! Don't miss this truth when you decide how to prioritize your missional responsibilities as a believer!

Chapter 5

The Power of Prayer-Propelled Evangelism

We have seen how the missional priority of reaching political leaders runs throughout the whole of the Bible. How believers achieve this missional priority is also provided for us in the Bible.

My New Testament Survey professor in seminary, the humble, respected, and prolific author, the late Dr. Robert Thomas, began class each day by praying for the salvation of our country's political leaders. At that point in my life, I hadn't yet discovered the truths I have just shared, and I asked him one day why he always prayed as he did.

"It's simple," he said. "It's just a matter of obedience to 1 Timothy 2:1–4 where we are told to prioritize this."

His reply made me all the more curious. And then he quoted 1 Timothy 2:3 from memory: *This* [an evangelistic prayer for political leaders] ***is good and acceptable in the sight of God our Savior.*** I now better understand what he meant, and I hope you do too.

> In that Paul first instructed Timothy to prioritize praying for the salvation of societies' political leaders, the same devotion to this principle should remain intact today.

In 1 Timothy 2:1 (NASB), Paul uses four words to elaborate on the specific kinds of evangelistic prayers to *be made in behalf of all people, for kings and all who are in authority.* These four descriptive, motivational words, when best understood, should compel our best efforts at evangelistic praying. The purpose of this chapter is to explain each of these four words in greater detail with a view as to how they should move believers to seek the lost in prayer and outreach.

REQUESTS (*DEESIS*)

The Greek root word *deesis* means "to lack, to be deprived; to be without something." Its use in the context of prayer in 1 Timothy 2:1 and elsewhere throughout the Scriptures carries the idea of an individual's realization of the needs of the lost. The believer is to pray, motivated by the fact that God will supply the sinner the remedy for his sin via speaking to his inner man about the cross of Christ. The enormity of the sinner's needs, i.e., that we are all sinners lacking and lost apart from the work of Christ on our behalf, should compel us to pray, requesting that God would touch each official with His grace and forgiveness and lead him to repentance and the way of salvation.

PRAYERS (*PROSEUCHE*)

The only use of this Greek word in Scripture relates to prayers to God of worship and reverence. The contextual idea is that when the sinner is converted through the work of the Holy Spirit as a result of evangelistic praying, that person's salvation brings great glory to God. Hence, we are motivated to pray evangelistic prayers because God is honored, worshipped, reverenced, and glorified when He miraculously reaches down into the hardened soul of a sinner and bestows upon that person the wonderful gift of new life in Christ!

Salvation is one hundred percent a work of God in the heart of every unregenerate person; therefore, when a sinner repents, God gets all the glory!

INTERCESSIONS (*ENTEUXIS*)

This Greek word appears in this verse and in only one other Scripture—1 Timothy 4:5—where the word is translated as *prayer* and means "to fall in with someone." The underlying idea is that a person involves himself in terms of understanding the sinner's plight. He does not pray for the lost with a cold, detached, mechanical attitude, but with love and concern regarding the person's future destiny.

THANKSGIVING (*EUCHARISTA*)

Lastly, in Paul's elaboration of the four motivational aspects to achieve evangelistic prayer, he states that all followers of Christ should be moved to pray for the lost because *it is a great privilege granted to the believer by God!* As **ambassadors for Christ** (2 Corinthians 5:20), every believer is given a role to play in the salvation of others. Exercising the privilege of leading another to Christ begins with **thankfulness** to God for the opportunity! That is the idea here and why it is included.

***

In summary, the believer is to go to God on behalf of ***all people, for kings and all who are in authority***, seeking their salvation and motivated by these four facets of intimacy with God. To recap, these four words should move believers to seek the lost in prayer and outreach:

- We *request* of Him because we are sensitive and in concert with the needs of the lost.
- We *pray* to Him and give Him glory because of His power to save.
- We *intercede* on behalf of the unregenerate because we are concerned for the future of the lost without Christ.
- We *thank* Him because we are grateful for the opportunity to witness on His behalf.

These insights should motivate believers to address God with evangelistic passion so as to achieve both the present and eternal results promised in 1 Timothy 2:1–4!

May these insightful aspects of communion with God inspire us to continually pray with sobriety and diligence!

It follows that Christians and churches should not only desire but also be committed first to evangelistic prayer, as well as to various ensuing outreaches and ministries to political leaders.

As seen throughout this chapter, such fervent, evangelistic praying for political leaders is biblically commanded of every believer! In chapter six, note now the promised multiple results.

Chapter 6

The National Benefits of This Missional Priority

I have refrained until the end of this part to explain the here-and-now benefits of obedience to this missional priority. These benefits are in addition to the efficiency and expediency aspects related to fulfilling the Great Commission.

God promises that if we obey Christ's command to first pray, then evangelize and disciple political leaders, something special will result. What follows is a wonderful chiastic structure of classic Pauline literary prose: the four aspects of evangelistic praying, i.e., ***requests, prayers, intercession, and thanksgiving***, are matched by the four parallel benefits that follow! Notice 1 Timothy 2:2b—*right in the middle of this passage but often overlooked*—with this idea in mind: ***so that we may lead a tranquil and quiet life in all godliness and dignity.***

Under the inspiration of the Holy Spirit, Paul is saying in prosaic language that *the four disciplines of prayer are blessed by four benefits of prayer*: **tranquil and quiet ... godliness and dignity!** Hopefully, you can now see why I spent so much time building the case for the disciplined prerequisite of prayer. Praying is necessary to achieve the *so that* benefits of prayer listed in the previous passage! Again, such praying is a matter not only of effectively fulfilling the Great Commission but also of making political leaders a missional priority to achieve magnificent results here and now in a nation!

Is not *a tranquil and quiet life in all godliness and dignity* a good summation of what every citizen desires both personally and for his nation? Is that not the essence of the American dream? *If so, then the preceding directive is God's formula for achieving such outward national blessings! Here is God's timeless prescription for building, maintaining, or restoring a nation!*

Most previous and present Christian leaders have viewed and continue to view the Church's primary role as one of lobbying civil government relative to moral issues. As we will see in Part II, such practices are the misguided "missional" priorities of Neo-evangelicalism and the Religious Right epochs of American Church history. Moralistic lobbying has its place and is necessary in a democratic republic such as America, but changing the direction of a nation is best accomplished by the Church when it has discipled those whom it sends into public office to work from the inside of the institution of civil government!

First Timothy 2:1–4 reveals the procedure—the biblically explicit formula—for Christians to *impact their nation most effectively* for good.

What results from evangelizing and
discipling governing authorities—states
the Word of God in this passage—is a

better nation! This is Scripture's cause-and-effect principle for nation building!

The Scripture contains many cause-and-effect formulas. Notice, for instance, the simple construction of Jesus' Beatitude, *"Blessed are those who hunger and thirst for righteousness, for they shall be satisfied"* (Matthew 5:6). In this case, satisfaction comes directly from pursuing righteousness. Satisfaction comes not from pursuing satisfaction but as a by-product of pursuing something else.

In a parallel sense, Scripture states that a nation characterized by *tranquility* in the citizenry results not from the pursuit of *tranquility* but from evangelizing and discipling those in authority. The passage states that concentrating on this pursuit leads to *a tranquil and quiet life in all godliness and dignity.* Therein is the cause-and-effect formula.

In a more practical sense, William Penn, one of America's Founding Fathers, illustrated this cause-and-effect relationship when he said in the Preface to the Frame of Government of the Colony of Pennsylvania, 1682: *Good hearts in lawmakers lead to good laws in society; whereas bad hearts in lawmakers lead to bad laws in society.*[4]

Practically speaking, the Church's executing this missional priority sets the tone for a nation. It therefore follows that political leaders need to receive preferential treatment in Church missiology!

Believers must reach political leaders at all levels of their career paths if any nation is to remain strong. We need to reach not only state and federal governing authorities but also local and county political leaders! Such a biblically based strategy will generate the maximum effect and outcome over time. May God illumine these truths to our hearts and guide our steps accordingly in the days ahead.

Praying evangelistically for those in authority is necessary to achieve *a tranquil and quiet life in all godliness and dignity.*

Therefore, I am including an in-depth study on each of these biblical words and their specific benefits.

TRANQUILITY, QUIETNESS, GODLINESS, AND DIGNITY

These four words chosen by the Apostle Paul in 1 Timothy 2:2 are worth pondering in greater depth if for no other reason than that they specifically identify the beneficial outcome both individually and corporately for those having disciplined themselves to follow Scripture and prioritize reaching political leaders for Christ.

These last four words of Paul's chiasm are all connected by and pivot on what is referred to as the *hina* clause in the Greek language, which is appropriately translated *in order that*. What wonderful causal effects are ours as a result of pursuing this missional priority! Why prayerfully and effectively evangelize *kings and all who are in authority*? *In order that we may lead ...* the four descriptive words that follow.

Tranquil

The Greek word used by Paul is unique to the whole of the New Testament, appearing in only one other place in the Greek translation of the Hebrew Old Testament (the Septuagint). Proverbs 14:30 states, *A tranquil heart is life to the body....* Solomon's use of the word *tranquil* means "a healthy, sound mind and emotions" in contrast to the following truism of the proverb: *But passion is rottenness to the bones.*

The word used for *passion* is the same root from which the English words "jealousy" and "ardor" are derived. Whereas internal *tranquility* results in external health, internal disruption destroys it. Accordingly, Paul is saying that part of the benefit of tranquility is physical health.

> In context, when a person is fortunate enough to live in a country characterized by higher degrees of peace and serenity and free from continual mental agitation, living with a corporate sense of steadiness and stability will generate greater physical health in the populace.

These words are descriptive of the kind of place where you and I and most everyone would want to live in order to raise a healthy family. Such an atmosphere, states 1 Timothy 2:2, results from evangelizing *kings and all who are in authority.*

Quiet

I find it fascinating to plumb the Pauline use of this word elsewhere in the New Testament. The same Greek root translated in this verse as the English word *quiet* is also found in 1 Thessalonians 4:11, which states, *and to make it your ambition to lead a quiet life and attend to your own business and work with your hands....*

Paul's use of the Greek word *quiet* has similar, interesting, and insightful *associations* in both of these passages and one that will follow. The three passages contain almost synonymous attributes of what living a *quiet* life in a country actually equates to. Saying that his use of the word is associated with and descriptive of a person's opportunity to pursue his dreams and the freedom to build his future via personal industry and initiative is by no means a stretch.

The third use of the word *quiet* appears in 2 Thessalonians 3:12, which says, *Now such persons we command and exhort in the Lord Jesus Christ to work in quiet fashion and eat their own bread.* Note from the second and third passages that this word is associated with *own business, own hands*, and *own bread*. Is it any wonder that those countries in which the furtherance of the gospel has affected governmental leadership and constitutional formation enjoy free enterprise where people can *own* possessions? The country savors a sense of contentment and personal prosperity to the same degree, generally speaking, that Christianity has taken hold in the hearts of the leaders of the land. The two go hand in hand. Paul equates these blessings with his usage of the word *quiet*.

Godliness

This word appears fifteen times in the New Testament and has the parallel meaning to "Christlikeness." "What would Jesus do?" is a popular phrase emblematic of *godliness*.

When the citizens pursue personal holiness and the political leaders themselves have been affected by the same gospel, the result will be an increasingly Christlike culture characterized by, among other attributes, the following:

- Provision for the needy
- Care for the unborn and the elderly
- Wise stewardship of the treasury
- Responsible and unhindered development of natural resources
- Clarity regarding gender identity
- Marriage between one man and one woman

Because the citizenry is godly, the culture subdues the earth, extracts its resources (by the sweat of their brow due to the Fall) with respect for the Creator's creation, and turns its God-given gift of raw materials into value-added beneficial products and services for the prosperity and well-being of all.

Following biblical instruction is how godly people in part manifest their *godliness* in the here and now. Praying for, evangelizing, and discipling political leaders creates a Christlike culture characterized by *godliness*.

Dignity

The repetitious use and idea of this word throughout Scripture carries with it the contextual specificity that people have intrinsic worth, will seek to live honorably, will have seriousness in their pursuits, and will be compelled to move forth by the sheer gravity of their being made in the image of God. In a world where political leaders and the citizenry are evangelized and, in their discipleship, understand that they are created in the image of God, there will exist a sense of *dignity*.

When evangelism and discipleship of political leaders occur, Paul says four benefits will inure to a society—and to its individual members—*that we may lead a tranquil and quiet life in all godliness and dignity*. This promise is for here and now!

* * *

An amazingly simple summary observation is in order. In the early days of the American Republic, during the Puritan period when our Founding Fathers were profoundly and forthrightly affected by their Christian faith, a higher degree of *tranquility, quietness, godliness, and dignity* (as previously defined) prevailed than presently exists.

Why? The Church had purposely affected the Founding Fathers with the faith. That infusion of faith fundamentally led to the creation of the greatest nation in history. Today the Church has shirked from this priority of its mission, and the results are clearly evident: America is increasingly spiraling downward in a rapid decline. All that to state this fact: *American Church history itself* illustrates this cause-and-effect relationship explicated by the Apostle Paul under the inspiration of the Holy Spirit in 1 Timothy 2:1–4!

SUMMARY

In summary, this inspired-by-God letter from the Apostle Paul to Timothy houses the main New Testament passage that buttresses the timeless principle of the cause-and-effect construction that I have elaborated on throughout Part I of this book.

> If one reaches political leaders for Christ,
> then the biblically promised effect in addition
> to the salvation of others and the more efficient
> fulfillment of the Great Commission is the
> changing of a nation in the here and now.

In order to capture the essence of this wonderful passage and its magnificent benefits more clearly, I want to make two additional critical observations about this passage:

First is the need to clarify that verse four informs verse one. Verse four states what kind of prayer Paul had in mind: ***who desires all people to be saved.*** The salvation of others is the context of the four aspects of prayers mentioned in verse one. Said in another way, verse one prayers are to have an eye toward salvation. *There is no getting around the overall context, i.e., the fact that Paul had evangelism in mind in these passages!* The relationship between verses one and four becomes even more evident when considering the second additional clarification.

An elementary principle of the Greek language needs to be stated for the reader to best understand the exclamatory fervor of the passage: *the antecedents to Greek pronouns, if not a previously listed person, are typically related to a noun clause connected to the main verb as opposed to an adverb clause.* That rule is a mouth full, so let me explain.

Such is the case in 1 Timothy 2:1–4 regarding the pronoun *this* at the beginning of verse 3:

> *First of all, then, I urge that requests, prayers, intercession, and thanksgiving be made in behalf of all people, for kings and all who are in authority, so that we may lead a tranquil and quiet life in all godliness and dignity. This is good and acceptable in the sight of God our Savior, who wants all people to be saved and to come to the knowledge of the truth* (NASB).

The pronoun *this* at the beginning of verse 3 refers to the noun clause acting as the direct object of the main verb in verse one about various kinds of evangelistic prayers *be*[ing] *made*. This insight and explanation is so important because what follows the word *this* in verse three *further elaborates* on the effect of various kinds of evangelistic prayers *be*[ing] *made* that are *good and acceptable in the sight of God our Savior*.

That is to say, what follows *this* is *not* a further elaboration on the immediately preceding clause: *so that we may lead a tranquil and quiet life in all godliness and dignity*. Rather, again, the pronoun relates to the noun clause acting as the direct object of the main verb—*be*[ing] *made*—not the subordinate clause acting as an adverb.

What specifically is said to be *good and acceptable in the sight of God* relates to the main idea of the passage, which is the key point of this book: evangelistic outreach to others (in general) and those in authority (in specific).

Various kinds of evangelistic prayers, which are *good and acceptable in the sight of God our Savior*, bring about the eternal effect of salvation (v. 4), as well as the here-and-now effect of *a tranquil and quiet life in all godliness and dignity* in a given society.

My point is, a formula is revealed within this passage that leads to these results, and that biblically revealed formula involves evangelizing the leaders of a nation!

Of course, with all of those benefits, it stands to reason that Paul, inspired by the Holy Spirit, would exclaim, *This is good and acceptable in the sight of God our Savior!* This exclamation was like using a font and enhancing it with the bold, italic, and underline features, even though those kinds of print fonts did not yet exist!

Perhaps you have read this chapter too quickly and are struggling with understanding this sentence construction. In order to better understand, what follows is a rearrangement of the passage with "the antecedent of the pronoun is the main verb—not the preceding clause" insight in mind:

> *First of all, then, I urge that requests, prayers, intercession, and thanksgiving be made in behalf of all people, for kings and all who are in authority, This* [evangelism/prayers being made] *is good and acceptable in the sight of God our Savior, who wants all people to be saved and to come to the knowledge of the truth… in order that* [the effect or result of the four aspects of evangelism/prayers] *we may lead a tranquil and quiet life in all godliness and dignity* (NASB).

This delineated construction serves to join together the main Pauline thoughts on prayer and to display the powerful cause-and-effect proposition of the passage more clearly for those reading it in the English language.

Summarily, the construction of this passage reveals that *in order* to have a nation characterized by *tranquility, quiet life, godliness and dignity*, believers need to evangelize not only the citizenry, but also *all who are in authority*.

These insights should create a better understanding of what Paul has said under the inspiration of the Holy Spirit as to the timeless biblical formula for building, preserving, or restoring a nation.

> Christians need to prioritize reaching political leaders for Christ in order to best fulfill the Great Commission and change their nation for the better.

Summarily, when the believer and the Church embrace reaching political leaders for Christ, at least three positive results take place:

1. The believer is personally blessed for obeying a vital tenet of the Word of God. *This is good and acceptable in the sight of God....*

2. The Great Commission is efficiently fulfilled. *Who desires all people to be saved....*

3. The restoration and preservation of the nation is gained. *So that we may lead a tranquil and quiet life....*

These three benefits are unmistakably evident from a close study of this passage.

At the risk of sounding overly negative, not only has the Church lost sight of its *specific* call to reach political leaders, but in America it has also bungled its call in a *general* sense to evangelize the masses. Part II will address that deficiency.

PART II

THE PREEMINENCE OF EVANGELISM AND DISCIPLESHIP AND THE ANALYSIS OF THE EPOCH OF A BUNGLING CHURCH

An exegetically based apologetic has been made in Part I relative to the priority of and ensuing benefits of reaching public servants for Christ. Part I makes it crystal clear that Scripture is replete with many examples of this directive. A strong case has been built for this irrefutable missional priority.

In this second part of the book, I will further the argument by building a historical apologetic—one based on American Church history. I will further make the case that the American Church has lost sight of the primacy of its institutional design not only in regard to specifically reaching **kings and all who are in authority** but in a general sense relative to reaching the whole of the nation.

It stands to reason that the degree to which the Church fulfills the primacy of its calling to evangelize and disciple the lost is the same degree to which it is a preserving and illuminating force in a fallen world and a given nation, i.e., salt and light respectively (cf. Matthew 5:13–14). Unfortunately, for many reasons, throughout the major epochs of American Church history, she has failed in fulfilling that specific task. In fact, her efforts to engage culture relative to her institutional purpose have been characterized by many clumsy mistakes. I submit that the Church in America is continually bungling her calling.

Bungling, which means "making or characterized by many clumsy mistakes," is, by and large, an appropriate encapsulation that best depicts the American Church's ineffectiveness in bringing about positive change in our deteriorating nation.

The second key word I have used in the titling of this second part is *epoch*, which *The Merriam-Webster Dictionary* defines as "a period of time in history or a person's life, typically one marked by notable events or particular characteristics."[1]

A historic overview of the five major epochs of American Church history will ferret out the various reasons why the Church has failed to make evangelism and discipleship her primary mission—not only as it relates specifically to public servants, but, in general, to the whole of the populace.

For nearly one-half of a century now in this fifth epoch of American Church history known as the Religious Right epoch, the American Church's major emphasis and involvement, specifically as it relates to Washington, D.C., has been largely characterized by attempts to change various laws of the land. Laws based in biblical precepts (in contrast to the enactment of laws that are untethered to scriptural precepts) are certainly important and worthy objectives, and many in office who name the name of Christ are heavily vested in that noble purpose.

But Scripture is clear in many passages that the preeminent calling and purpose intended by God relative to His institution of the Church is to fulfill the Great Commission and to build the body of Christ by winning and discipling the lost. This intention is made clear in the following passages: Matthew 28:19–20 and Ephesians 4:11–12.

In fact, in Luke chapter 3, God's Word reveals and exemplifies the importance of this aforementioned focus and discipline as it relates to changing the direction of a nation, i.e., combatting societal deterioration.

In Luke 3:3–14 God's intended means to change a culture is on display.

Over the past 45 years in this Religious Right epoch of American Church history, Evangelical church pastors and leaders have strongly debated how believers should best engage in societal preservation and illumination. The urgency of this heated discussion is anticipatable given America's rapidly increasing moral decline. Rightfully so, the Church has asked herself, "How can this ship be turned around?"

This very topic was my main focus of study during my eight years of seminary training. While I want to believe that both sides of the societal change debate represent noble motives and seek the same objective, how to best achieve that goal remains controversial. The ensuing passages make a strong and simple case for the following:

> The believer's emphasis on heart change will assuredly result in law and societal change.

Embracing "heart change" is to embrace the long game, whereas to embrace "law change" tempts the believer with the promise of quicker results. However, these results may not be achievable or even sustainable due to the essence and very nature of the political process in a democratic republic form of civil government.

Chapter 7

The Social Implications of John the Baptist's Evangelism

The third chapter of Luke is a profoundly insightful passage regarding this debate, *exemplifying the guaranteed social benefits that inure to a country where and when the Church prioritizes heart change via evangelism and discipleship.* The following excerpts from that somewhat lengthy passage will enable you to quickly see my point.

Contextually in this passage, the "he" is John the Baptist who precedes the earthly ministry of Jesus Christ. He was an evangelist who preached the need to repent as a necessary component to receiving Christ. Otherwise, when you think about it, why do you need to be saved if in your heart there is no acknowledgment of being lost?[2] Other than possessing a strong sense of inner conviction regarding personal lostness, why would you genuinely and volitionally seek Christ and His forgiveness?

And he came into all the district around the Jordan, preaching a baptism of repentance for the forgiveness of sins (v. 3).

"Therefore bear fruits in keeping with repentance...." (v. 8).

And the crowds were questioning him, saying, "Then what shall we do?" And he would answer and say to them, "The man who has two tunics is to share with him who has none; and he who has food is to do likewise." And some tax collectors also came to be baptized, and they said to him, "Teacher, what shall we do?" And he said to them, "Collect no more than what you have been ordered to." Some soldiers were questioning him, saying, "And what about us, what shall we do?" And he said to them, "Do not take money from anyone by force, or accuse anyone falsely, and be content with your wages" (vv. 10–14).[3]

I have purposefully positioned the passage in order to emphasize, clarify, and simplify its read in a way that makes the social implications of John's evangelism immediately apparent. All were profoundly affected by John's preaching and possessed an internal Holy Spirit-driven curiosity and unction characterized by and resulting in the same question: *"What shall we do?"*

The large crowd that John drew represented much of society. Luke identifies the first of the three cultural sectors in verses 10 and 11 as **the multitudes**. The second curious sector identified in verses 12 and 13 were the **tax gatherers** who assisted the occupying Romans, and the third segment mentioned in verse 14 was **some soldiers** (Jewish soldiers most likely).

Before providing a brief examination of each sector, it is important to note that John the Baptist is not preaching that these people give up their professions. As a side note, the Pharisees regarded these last professions to be questionable. Rather, the Baptist instructed the people to behave honorably and honestly in these occupations.[4]

This distinction is important to recognize: in each of the three cases, John the Baptist is preaching that conversion should lead to the betterment of society. Those who are converted to Christ will turn from their former sinful ways and lead lives pleasing to God. *The implication in this passage is that true repentance will always result in a certain form of behavioral and societal change.* An examination of these groups one at a time is in order for greater understanding.

THE MULTITUDES

John told these commoners who were curious regarding the implications of repentance and conversion, **"The man who has two tunics is to share with him who has none; and he who has food is to do likewise."** A tunic was customarily worn under a person's outer garment for extra warmth. Sometimes two were worn or an individual had an extra one. This instruction serves to illustrate the principle *"Love your neighbor as yourself,"* as taught by Moses in Leviticus 19:18 and by Jesus in Matthew 19:19.

Accordingly, the first illustration of the implication of repentance and salvation is that we will love others like we love ourselves. In Philippians 2 Paul says, *regard one another as more important than yourselves* (v. 3b). The societal change stemming from an individual's conversion is obvious from this passage. What a great world this would be if everyone practiced this ethic in culture!

THE JEWISH TAX GATHERERS

Tax gatherers, who were perceived to have sold their soul to the occupying Roman forces, were despised and hated by their fellow countrymen. In fact, prior to his conversion, Mathew, the Gospel writer and disciple of Jesus Christ, had served as a Jewish *tax gatherer*. Often, those serving as publicans would exact a tax that was far beyond the profit margin necessary to stay in business yet allowed by their Roman franchisor.

John the Baptist herein addresses this very matter. He says to the onlooker who is counting the cost of coming to Christ, *"Collect no more than what you have been ordered to"* (v. 13b).

In a parallel instruction in 1 Thessalonians 2:5, Paul reminds the Thessalonian believers, *For we never came with flattering speech, as you know, nor with a pretext for greed....* Greed, which is characteristic of selfish, fallen individuals, is often the motivation for the exploitation of others. John has just instructed the multitudes, *Love your neighbors.* In today's vernacular, he is now saying to the *tax gatherers*, "Don't rip off your neighbors."

Here then is another cultural implication of repentance and conversion: the curtailment of *greed*. When a person comes to Jesus, He fills the void, recharacterizing a person's inner being. Someone who is filled with Christ is not in constant want. What a different place this world this would be if Psalm 23:1 were true of everyone: *The Lord is my shepherd, I shall not want.*

THE SOLDIERS

The last of the three illustrative groups that Luke records are the *soldiers* who came to John the Baptist. Most commentators agree that these were Jewish soldiers who provided protection and enforcement for the Jewish *tax gatherers*.[5] John is literally instructing them not to extort money by violence. The Greek word he uses means "not to shake violently."

If you are coming to Christ and desire His Lordship in and over your life, it means you won't "shake down" people anymore! John tells the powerful in society that if they desire to follow Christ, they will no longer misuse their power to take advantage of others, but rather *be content with* [their] *wages*.[6]

What a different place this world would be if people loved their neighbors as themselves, didn't seek to rip them off in some way, nor abused them. Luke 3 serves to illustrate God's intended means to achieve long-lasting, real societal change by leading others to repentance and faith in Christ!

Luke 3 is a powerful passage that serves to illustrate the pragmatic implications of societal betterment that stem from an institutional Church solely focused on soul conversion! Don't miss this instruction from the passage: each individual representing the three segments of culture is instructed by John to bear character qualities that will most certainly benefit society!

Again and again, it is very simple to see from the redundancy of the passage, soul conversion is the best way for believers to effect societal change in the long run. To act out with other priorities in order to attempt to change the direction of a deteriorating nation is to disagree with this simple, clear narrative passage.

In Ephesians 2, the Apostle Paul declaratively states the same precept that Luke has illustrated via the life and preaching ministry of John the Baptist. Prior to coming to Christ, [we] *were dead in* [our] *trespasses and sins, in which* [we] *formerly walked* (2:1). *We too all formerly lived in the lusts of our flesh, indulging the desires of the flesh and of the mind, and were by nature children of wrath ...* (2:3).

But to those who have repented and are regenerate in Christ, Paul states the following in Ephesians 5:8–9, *you were formerly darkness, but now you are Light in the Lord; walk as children of Light (for the fruit of the Light consists in all goodness and righteousness and truth).* The sequence of both Luke's Scripture and Paul's passages serves to illustrate the contrasting nature between those who are unregenerate versus the repentant who have bowed the knee, come to Christ (cf. John 1:12), and are now baptized in, strengthened by, and empowered with His Holy Spirit (cf. Acts 2; Ephesians 5:18).

Many other parallel passages exist that make this same point. Evangelizing the lost is the biblically revealed means by which the

Church is to go about changing culture. What follows, however, will provide you with a more profound understanding as to how the American Church has *repeatedly* bungled its calling. In fact, it has bungled its calling—the simple message that John the Baptist and the Apostle Paul herein heralded—in every major epoch of its history!

In its attempt to change the country by focusing on better laws, American Evangelicalism[7] has discounted and woefully underemphasized the power of what John the Baptist and the Apostle Paul illustrated and proclaimed: evangelism! And look at what has happened: the nation has only become worse. Sadly, the country has not changed for the better.

In the past 45 years of attempting to change laws more so than hearts, the Christian activist movement has little to show for its efforts. The country is increasingly secular and increasingly sticking its finger in the eye of God.

> Would you agree with me that the time has come for believers to make evangelism a priority in the political arena?

With the diminishment of the Religious Right movement in recent years, the time is now to discover, commit to, and emphasize the simple biblical formula for effecting societal change as illustrated in Luke chapter 3 and the book of Ephesians.

What follows is a brief history evidencing the repetition of this lack of a Luke 3 emphasis in American Church history. A broader historical perspective relative to this important topic will help believers shape a better-informed, deep-seated conviction going forward as it relates to the preeminence of evangelism not only to build God's kingdom in heaven but also to produce societal change in our nation.

It follows that if the Church can't grasp this missional principle related to ***all people*** in a *general* sense, it cannot be expected to apply it in a *specific* sense to **kings and all who are in authority**.

Chapter 8

1776:
The Puritan Pulpit
Shapes American Culture

Postmillennialism was the prevailing eschatological point of view of the American Church from the Puritan era through the Civil War. *Postmillennialism* is the Christian view that Christ will return at the end of the millennial period that is described in the book of Revelation. The Postmillennialists believe that, by this time, the Church will have "Christianized" the world and will have prepared the way for Him. This belief was the predominant singular motivation that explains why Protestants were so involved in societal change during this earliest period of American Church history. Postmillennialism was promoted through this period of the Great Awakening by such preachers as Jonathan Edwards.

> In this context, the Church was largely motivated by a prophetic determinism as it pertained to societal change; accordingly, the postmillennial-driven Church directly attached itself to culture and politics.

Such involvement was essential to ushering in the kingdom, which is only logical in that, per the tenets of Postmillennialism, Christ will *only* return when believers have prepared the way by "Christianizing" all the nations of the world. In Postmillennial thought, Christianizing the world is "the believer's side of the bargain" that must be achieved in order to enact Christ's Second Coming. To illustrate the tangential fervor of Postmillennial belief in early America, Church historian George Marsden summarizes what was widely believed at that time:

> America has a special place in God's plans and will be the center for the great spiritual and moral reform that will lead to the golden age or "millennium" of Christian civilization. Moral reform accordingly is crucial for hastening this spiritual millennium.[8]

The Puritans believed that Christ's kingdom would grow out of the spiritual and moral progress gained by and through the believer's efforts at reforming politics and culture in the present age. That belief is held today by Postmillennialists who are also known as Dominion Theologians, Theonomists, Christian Reconstructionists, and also by the latest secular media descriptor, "Christian Nationalism."[9] But importantly, notice that reforming is not necessarily equated with soul winning, i.e., the explicit formula and result of Luke chapter 3 evangelism.

Arthur Cushman McGiffert, a leading Postmillennialist, stated, "The kingdom of God is not a kingdom lying in another world beyond the skies but established here and now,"[10] which accurately serves to further illustrate the summation of this belief. Accordingly, missionary progress was measured during the Puritan period not only in terms of evangelistic crusades, revivals, and church planting, but also in terms of cultural advancement. Cultural successes pertaining to slavery, abolition, and technological achievement were as much measurements of the "Christianization" of America as anything else.

The point is that before Theological Liberalism (the next epoch to be addressed) intruded into the Church after the Civil War, most Christians actively engaged in the culture and in politics to prepare the world for Christ's Second Coming. This thinking characterized Postmillennialism and was the singular prevailing theological impetus that motivated, wedded, and justified the Church's emphasis and direct involvement in the politics and the culture of the country. Whether this is a model that today's Evangelical church should employ for similar success depends upon a careful exegetical examination to determine whether Postmillennialism eschatology is scriptural in the first place.

In fact, Postmillennialism is not exegetically popular today; the doctrine has been roundly discounted by leading conservative Evangelical theologians. In the late twentieth and now twenty-first century, the increasingly popular eschatology in the American Church has been Premillennialism. In vast contrast to Postmillennialism, this eschatological camp believes that Christ's Second Coming will occur at the start of the millennial period in order to save the world from its own demise and tragedy. Most of today's leading national Evangelical expository radio preachers are Premillennialists. This argument is biblically defensible, but arguing for this viewpoint herein is beyond the scope of this book.[11] Accordingly:

> Postmillennialism is in no position to be the *tour de force* that it once was

> so as to be a leading impetus and
> motivation for cultural change today.

That deficiency of Postmillennialism is that there is no Scripture to support the idea that Christ's Second Coming depends on the Church's "Christianizing" culture beforehand. Postmillennialism, also known as "prophetic determinism," is a convenient, pragmatic, motivational way to engage believers in culture but is woefully lacking in terms of exegetical/biblical support.

In other words, any basis for the Church's sustainable social involvement depends upon its being biblically substantiative.[12] To be clear, if the premise of Postmillennialism is built on a faulty eschatology (by the way, it was rejected by the American Church by the conclusion of World War II), it therefore stands to reason that what motivated Puritan cultural involvement then is something other than a simple Luke 3 impetus.

To summarize this first epoch of American Church history, it follows that for today's Church to be motivated in similar ways to better society, it would have to re-adopt a faulty eschatology that has already by in large been rejected.[13]

The formula that served to engage the early American Church in a mission to better society was motivated by Postmillennial eschatology per se, versus a Luke 3 understanding of the results of evangelism.

Chapter 9

1877:
The Encroachment of Theological Liberalism

The period in American Church history that immediately followed Puritanism was the rise of Theological Liberalism, also known as Modernism or the Social Gospel. This changing of the guard was a dominant (but not entire) metamorphosis that occurred over a period of time from approximately 1865 to 1915. This movement predominantly transformed Postmillennial-driven Puritanism into liberal Protestantism and ushered in what is commonly referred to as the emergence of a Social Gospel form of "Christianity."

During this period of American Church history, there can be no doubt as to the accelerating involvement of the American "Church" in the political/social arena as depicted by the synonymous name the *Social Gospel*. The more pertinent question, however, is the following question: Was the Social Gospel form of Christianity a biblical Christianity, or, for that matter, was it Christianity at all?

J. Gresham Machen stated resoundingly, "No, it is not." After his book *Christianity & Liberalism* was published in 1923, Machen became the chief spokesman against what had become a thoroughly established liberal Protestantism. Machen (from whose primer I learned the Greek language) had been a New Testament professor at Princeton Theological Seminary before the theologically liberal Presbyterians wrested control of the institution.

Machen and his theologically conservative cohorts then left the school to found Westminster Seminary. Importantly and accurately, he insisted that liberal Protestantism was "another religion, since it proposed an entirely new view of Jesus and a scheme of salvation other than Christianity had ever taught before."[14] Machen was accurate in his analysis, and I will attempt to summarize his thinking as follows:

> In essence, America had birthed another religion and called it the same name. The "Church" of the Social Gospel changed Scripture in order to change culture.

Liberal Protestantism had escaped the confines of Christianity's irreducible minimums. The core heresy of liberal theology continues to be this: Jesus is not our Savior; He is merely a humble, humanitarian role model, a good example we should emulate—as if this description is all that Jesus is about! Herein is a satanic stripping away and a denuding of the power of the cross of Christ. Theological Liberals do not believe Christ is the Savior, nor do they believe that man's wretched, sin-laden, fallen soul needs saving.

Modernism represented a not-so-subtle convergence of four concussive influences on Puritan Christianity, which I will briefly explain.

1. Modernism was composed of Naturalism or Darwinism, which raised doubt as to the supernatural and scientific accuracy of Scripture.

2. Modernism contained within it the presupposition of human rationalism. That is to say that man's reasoning was deemed superior to God's revelation in Scripture. Therefore, whatever in Scripture could not be understood through man's reasoning (which is finite and fallen, I might add; this is called the noetic effect of sin) was viewed with suspicion.

3. Historical Criticism was imported from the Tubingen School in Germany. This kind of criticism had many forms, with the intellectual intent of casting doubt, among other things, on the accuracy of the Synoptic Gospels, which are the Gospels written from a similar point of view by Matthew, Mark, and Luke. It asked the following question: Can the believer trust what Matthew, Mark, and Luke wrote? This criticism questioned whether the historical Jesus was different from the "Christian" Jesus whom the Gospel writers had portrayed and embellished.

    In this sense, the German "intellectuals" from the School of Tubingen exported their belief that the Scriptures were tainted with theoretical plausible doubt through both Naturalism and Historical Criticism, which is the science of codifying the ancient manuscript evidence in the manufacture of the Bible.

4. Add the fourth influence of the encroaching Social Gospel as invented by Kant, Schleiermacher, and Beecher, and "Christianity" had degenerated into nothing more than a moral code for people to live by. Liberal Protestantism was—and remains—a far cry from biblical Christianity.

As an aside, this decay explains why so many who say they are "Christians" in the Capitol are, in fact, embedded in the false "christianity" of Theological Liberalism and, therefore, reason differently on policy issues.

As Machen quipped:

> They may wear the name "Christian"
> on their shirtsleeve—but they are
> part of another religion![15]

How can we best understand such a *radical* theological shift in a relatively short period of time—from a culturally predominant, nationally controlling conservative Puritanism to a runaway Liberal Protestantism as the *tour de force* in American culture? During this profoundly important-to-understand period of what I'll call "American Church theological transformation," the traditional theologically conservative theologians mounted a negligible defense of the true biblically based Christian faith.

The lionhearted rhetoric of William F. Warren, the president of Boston University, provides insight to the fact that conservative Christian leaders were pridefully asleep at the wheel. Notice this indictment in his words:

> Toward the middle of the last century came the fullness of God's time for generating a new Christian nationality.... [Now] all these threatening surges of Antichristian thought ... have come to us from European seas; not one arose in our own hemisphere....[16]

Conservative Christian leadership of the time either included few apologists of learning, or they made light of the threat until it was too late. They were reluctant to *BE ANGRY* in the justifiable sense of

Ephesians 4:26, of manifesting appropriate righteous indignation and mounting an aggressive rejection of encroaching false doctrine.

This attitude is descriptive of the great evangelist D. L. Moody, who was opposed to controversy itself. Whereas the New Testament writer Jude preempted his soteriological emphasis in order to earnestly defend the faith from apostasy in verse 3, Moody, who possessed the platform and the influence to do so in the American Church as a leading evangelist, would have no part in such activities. He was known as a theological pragmatist and "often tested doctrines relative to their suitability for evangelism."[17] He always sought peace and avoided controversy, seeking a "religion of the heart versus a religion of the mind."[18] He often dialogued with Theological Liberals, giving them grace with the hope that they would eventually come around and embrace biblical views. But such was not the case. As a result, in part, the Social Gospel brand of "christianity" became well-rooted as the primary theology and cultural force in America at that time.

> When all was said and done, the Social Gospel had eclipsed the Puritan pulpit as the major influence in American culture. But again, the "church" of the Social Gospel had changed Scripture in order to change culture.

For certain, the Church was now engaged in societal change but was far from being the true Church that embodied the great doctrines of the New Testament.

The previous four concussive influences now had similar weight if not greater prominence than did singular, simple biblical exposition. With the emergence of Theological Liberalism, the Bible was not the only source that informed Christian belief.

It therefore follows that the Modernists' justification for social action by citing Scripture is largely illegitimate because they truncate the basic doctrines of biblical Christianity in order to achieve their Social Gospel ends. The historic doctrines of the faith were reworked and modified into a counterfeit foundation for social aims. Theological Liberals are Scripture twisters. Make no mistake: Scripture does not justify the Social Gospel—much of the Social Gospel seeks to replace Scripture. Therefore, Scripture does not validate the political/social direction of Modernism because the Social Gospel is not a substantiated manifestation of biblical Christianity to begin with! More importantly, it is antithetical to it!

Eisegetical means "to read one's opinions into." Modernism was founded upon a self-styled eisegetical epistemology which seeks to morph and twist Scripture in order to use it to support preconceived liberal societal views. This view contrasts greatly with the objective use of Scripture, which is motivated by a desire to extract from it and apply its timeless, immutable precepts.

Accordingly, this period of Church history does not have a legitimate, extracted-from-Scripture, theological treatise to biblically justify its societal expression. Christian involvement in the political arena through this epoch of American Church history is found wanting of an accurate biblical and theological underpinning. The formula for cultural change as presented in Luke chapter 3 was far from its agenda because Theological Liberalism was and remains about social wokeness versus Luke chapter 3 personal evangelism.

For example, nowhere in the New Testament is there a command for the institution of the State to take care of the poor. At the risk of sounding heartless, in a careful study of Scripture relative to this politically divisive issue, the Bible teaches that the stewardship responsibility for the truly bereft in society lies at the feet of the individual, the family, and the institution of the Church in that order of priority. Social Gospellers would have people think otherwise, but they possess no scriptural basis for their viewpoint. According to Scripture, theirs is a faulty theology.

Conclusively, since Christ was not salvific to their way of thinking to begin with, the epoch of Theological Liberalism was void of a Luke 3 understanding of how to change a nation. What about the coming Fundamentalist period? Would it be characterized by the primacy of saving faith to create societal change?

Chapter 10

1920: The Fundamentalist Reaction

One of the recurring themes in Joel Carpenter's classic book, *Revive Us Again: The Reawakening of American Fundamentalism*, is the idea that the Fundamentalist movement's social involvement was motivated out of reactionary pride to take back the center stage from the Modernists who had stolen it from the Puritans. This fervency of cause was the predominant motive, a much stronger motive in this epoch than was a Luke 3 motive.

States Carpenter:

> Those who founded the Fundamentalist movement witnessed this shift in cultural leadership and began to notice that their own status and influence was waning.[19]

Earlier in his book he states:

> [They saw] their status as community leaders and the influence of their evangelical values decrease sharply while a new elite of university-trained secular professors and liberal clergy gained power and prestige.... Fundamentalists had been deeply shamed in the battles of the 1920s, but they could not give up on the vision of a Christian America.[20]

The human desire to retrieve all that had been lost to the liberals, i.e., seminaries, colleges, denominations, churches, mission agencies, publishing companies, and the like, was a compelling motive that seemed to eclipse the need for a clearly reasoned and biblical theology relative to how to go about best accomplishing that retrieval. This same compelling desire created the need to stop and question the validity of the motivation of a faulty Postmillennial eschatology. Furthermore, an underlying assumption by the Fundamentalists existed that what had been lost was that which God had intended for believers to get back and always possess.

Again, how the movement should go about biblically achieving repossession of these institutions is missing from the literature of the time. Accordingly, Fundamentalists sought many means to "take back America from the liberals," but during this period, no biblically reasoned document by any leader exists that shows how that objective should or could be achieved.

Fundamentalists were motivated and driven, if not captivated, by an overwhelming reactionary pragmatism to recover their huge losses. Given man's fallen nature, his inclination is understandable, even post-salvation, but not justifiable.

One of the chief intellectual spokespersons for Fundamentalism (although he did not identify himself as a Fundamentalist) was, as previously mentioned, J. Gresham Machen. Importantly, Machen argued against Fundamentalist political/social involvement that was intended to change culture.[21] Machen believed it was too easy for the Church, when focused on means other than evangelism and discipleship, to lapse into a moralizing campaign void of a biblical justification. In essence he foresaw the error of the fifth epoch in American Church history.

"Why try to take back that aspect of Theological Liberalism?" he reasoned. Machen alluded to this question when he said,

> The Christian Missionary...his chief business, he believes, is the saving of souls, and souls are saved not by [teaching] the mere ethical principles of Jesus but by His redemptive work...human goodness [the emphasis of Theological Liberalism] will avail nothing for lost souls; ye must be born again.[22]

Theological Liberals had united with the institution of the State in order to forward a false gospel that salvation was not through the simultaneous God-empowered actions of repentance and faith in Christ, which are the basis of solid, historical, biblically-driven Christianity, but rather by means of a Social Gospel. They taught that social redemption is what Jesus and the Bible are all about—not what the Bible actually says it's about—personal redemption.

Thus, the Fundamentalists reasoned that the reaction of the legitimate Christian to such aberrancy was to *withdraw from all forms of civil governmental involvement*. Second Corinthians 6:17 was a passage used to justify such separatist actions: **"Come out from their midst and be separate,"** says the Lord. **"And do not touch what is unclean...."** For sure, the *militant Fundamentalist did not want to be perceived as a Modernist*! This reactionary, summarily incorrect decision to withdraw from the political arena would have a devastating effect on the future of America.

The Fundamentalist, who understood and believed in the power of change via personal conversion to Christ, who understood and believed in the power of change via personal conversion to Christ, held a Luke chapter 3 understanding of societal change, and possessed the unadulterated message and doctrine of salvation had a knee-jerk reaction to ever being remotely associated with the heretical Social Gospellers and retreated from the mission field of the State! Summarily:

> Whereas the Puritans were intrinsically intertwined with the State, the reactionary Fundamentalists now abandoned it!

The Fundamentalists held a proper understanding of how best to achieve societal change in the sense of Luke chapter 3 and Ephesians (and the other parallel passages listed in the end notes)—that coming to Christ for salvation would internally change a sinner and result in his becoming a good citizen. But they abandoned the mission field of civil government to distance themselves from the Modernists.

Stemming from this knee-jerk reaction, Fundamentalists adopted an attitude of "politics is dirty." To this day, many Fundamentalist pastors want nothing to do with governmental involvement. How tragic! (Many of the elected leaders with whom I counsel experience this ostracism, and they ask me about it, wondering why. The information in the previous paragraphs greatly aids our understanding of this matter.)[23] Based on Scripture, both the Theological Liberals' promotion of the Social Gospel and the Fundamentalists' withdrawal from politics represent differing forms of faulty theology.

In our search across American Church history for the application of the simple truth of Luke chapter 3—that saving faith is the best progenitor of societal advance—let us recap:

A SUMMATION OF THE FIRST THREE EPOCHS

- The Puritans engaged culture motivated by Postmillennialism more so than personal evangelism.
- The Modernists engaged culture motivated by a social understanding of Jesus, not personal evangelism.
- The Fundamentalists did not engage culture even though they believed wholeheartedly that personal evangelism was the way to change it.

Chapter 11

1950: The Birth of Neo-evangelicalism

During the late 1940s, Harold Ockenga and Carl Henry, among others, established Neo-evangelicalism with the intent of "sanding off" the seemingly rough edges of an increasingly sectarian, militant Fundamentalism. By this time Fundamentalism had been bloodied in its war with liberal Protestantism, and its resulting public image was one of combativeness, which in simple terms had marginalized its influence in the eyes of a broad society.

Accordingly, "Neo-evangelical" was coined—a new title to a movement and a new desire to, among other objectives, increase Evangelical influence in society. Motivated by the belief that Fundamentalism had isolated itself from playing a major role in the influence of American culture, the purveyors of Neo-evangelicalism attempted a "Christian religion metamorphosis"—a makeover or, if you will, a resetting, a reintroduction of biblical Christianity. This "new chapter" idea can be illustrated in several ways.

First is the landmark article that appeared in *Christian Life* magazine in March 1956 titled, "Is Evangelical Theology Changing?" Contributors to the article were numerous noted Christian leaders. Among the eight listed major changes from Fundamentalism to Neo-evangelicalism was the need to have "a more definite recognition of social responsibility."[24] The article states in this regard:

> Nevertheless—unlike Fundamentalism—Neo-evangelicalism realizes the Church has a prophetic mission to society. There are times when the Church must thunder, "Thus saith the Lord!"[25]

The article goes on to say in greater specificity, "We must...make Evangelicalism more relevant to the political and sociological realities of our time."[26] But important to this book's thesis, the article fails to build a biblical basis or a means to accomplish the aforementioned conclusive statement. It follows that Carl Henry does not cite the simplicity of what John the Baptist is stating in Luke chapter 3; in fact, to do so would counter his argument.

Carl Henry, the leading voice in the Neo-evangelical movement, is known for his prominent work titled *The Uneasy Conscience of Modern Fundamentalism*. This book represents the Magna Carta of the Neo-evangelical position as the emerging movement attempted a pendulum swing away from the historically militant Fundamentalism. It is important to note this big-picture thesis when examining Henry's overall reactionary argumentation.

From a sense of logic and reasoning, Henry's postulations seem quite persuasive. However, he again fails to provide any sort of biblical basis for his thesis regarding the necessity of a social emphasis by the Church. Sadly, his thesis for Neo-evangelicalism's engagement in culture is not based on Luke chapter 3. *As a matter of fact, again and again, the simple formula of Luke 3 is nowhere to be found in Henry's book!*

This omission is hugely unfortunate because, in this next major epoch of American Church history, the Church will once again miss the biblical way in which it should primarily—and the way in which it is best suited in terms of its overall equipping and effectiveness—relate to and positively affect the State!

When Henry makes the charge that "Modern Fundamentalism does not explicitly sketch the social implications of its message for the non-Christian world," he is correct as it relates to Fundamentalism's abject withdrawal from the political arena. What Henry and his movement are about to do is turn the Church in a direction that once again fails to singularly prioritize and play its strong suit of evangelism!

> **Without its focus on the primacy of evangelism, the Church's attempt to change the State will prove largely powerless and ineffective.**

Many more voices of founding Neo-evangelical influence that advocated social-political change via the Church in ways other than its God-commissioned means of evangelism could be cited. Important to note, however, is this: even though one of the major tenets of Neo-evangelicalism is social involvement and reform, similar to the emphasis of Theological Liberalism (but without its doctrinal heresy), *the leaders provided no scriptural basis as justification for social involvement of the Church.* This absence is evident in The Lausanne Covenant itself![27] Unfortunately for the nation, Neo-evangelicalism failed to realize and manifest the simple truths of Luke chapter 3, and so America continued to slide.

Chapter 12

1975:
The Birth of
the Religious Right

The Evangelicals' attempts to change the cultural direction of America through political involvement perhaps bloomed more fully in the mid-1970s than ever before. Fundamentalist pastor Jerry Falwell founded *The Moral Majority*.[28] Thereafter televangelist Pat Robertson took the mantle of leadership via the auspices of his moralizing Christian organization, *The Christian Coalition*, founded in the mid-1980s and led by Ralph Reed. And then about ten years later, *Focus on the Family's* Dr. James Dobson assumed the baton. The latter's organization published the book, *Why You Can't Stay Silent: A Biblical Mandate to Shape Our Culture*.[29]

I should first preface what I am about to state with this statement: the late Dr. Falwell was a good friend of mine, as are Dr. Robertson and Dr. Dobson to this day. I love and respect these men dearly. *Focus on the Family's* book (Dr. Dobson is no longer with *Focus on the Family*) was the first major attempt to provide a biblical basis for cultural involvement in the political arena by Evangelicals, but again and unfortunately, nothing is said about a Luke chapter 3 emphasis and the three simple yet profound examples of the relationship between evangelism and societal change that are recorded in the passage. Rather, the book lapses into a supposed theology to justify a primacy for moralistic activism.

Certainly, the Church should have a prophetic voice, but when that prophetic voice is void of an overarching Luke 3 emphasis, the Church becomes nothing more than a moralizing agent. Why is it we can't seem to get this directive correct? *Why do we keep missing what Luke chapter 3 says is the way to go about this?*

From one epoch of American Church history to another, we, the American Evangelical movement as a whole, can't seem to land on the simplicity of what the Bible teaches regarding how the Church best influences a nation for good. This is not rocket science. The late Billy Graham and his ministry, the *Billy Graham Evangelistic Association*, is probably the best illustration of a ministry that did get this directive right. Billy Graham's unwavering commitment to soul winning best illustrates the Luke 3 principle.

> **If we can't get the *general* mission right (Part II), is it any wonder why we can't get the *specific* mission right (Part I)?**

This part of *All in Authority* encapsulates the five major epochs of American Church history as they relate to this subject. Luke chapter 3 is the way the Church is to engage in culture, but for one reason or another, the centrality of a Luke 3 priority is missing in all five epochs!

Make no mistake, the way the Church must relate to the State is via the primacy of evangelism and discipleship! The State desperately needs what the Church has to offer. The State is not in the business of generating righteous leaders and is therefore dependent on the Church to manufacture righteous leaders for it. But the Church never seems to give the State all the leaders it needs! Shame on us believers for not serving the State in a biblically correct manner!

Motivated primarily by Postmillennialism, the Puritans evangelized out of necessity. And because they did, America was founded with a dynamism and power unmatched in world history.

> Today we in the United States still ride the wave of evangelistic success brought about through the beliefs and actions of our Founding Fathers. The Puritan epoch had it right—even though their eschatological motivation for doing so was incorrect.

But that tsunami of the Puritan influence has abated greatly over the years due to all of the following epochs of American Church history simply because subsequent believers have lacked in implementing the primacy of evangelism and discipleship.

- Theological Liberals abandoned solid, biblical doctrine as they sought to influence America with a gospel of their own manufacture.
- Fundamentalists had the gospel right but retreated from culture.
- In their attempt to right the wrong of Fundamental sectarianism, Neo-evangelicals still failed in that their solution neglected to include the primacy and simplicity of evangelism.

- And the Religious Right movement, although full of sincere passion to right the ship, overlooked the simplicity and focus of evangelism, substituting in its place the complexity of governmental policy change. And though commendable and necessary in a "we the people" nation, such an emphasis is not as powerful and lasting as is calling people to repentance and new life in Christ—like John the Baptist did.

SUMMARY

When the Church disciples the new believer and sends him or her into leadership positions within the institution of the State, it is doing what it does best! After all, the Church is the only institution that can serve the State in this way. As Charles Colson said, the Church needs to be *pre-political* as its means to change a nation. When a person repents and receives the indwelling Holy Spirit, he cannot help but become a good citizen and a benefit to society, which is what Luke 3:10–18 is all about! Again, and to the thesis of this book, note the following:

> **If American Church history reveals a repeated failure in a *general* sense to emphasize its calling to evangelize and disciple the masses, is it any wonder why, in a *specific* sense, it would fail to prioritize the same to its political leaders?**

Will the next epoch of American Church history—one that I believe is about to begin—be characterized by the primacy and simplicity of evangelism relative to the State, or will this biblically informed emphasis be somehow missed once again, placing an aberrant prominence on social justice or some other fad?

We desperately need churches and church members to evangelize their neighbors and political leaders alike—exactly like Jesus tells the Apostle Paul to do in Acts 9:15 and Paul likewise instructs Pastor Timothy to do in 1 Timothy 2:1–4!

May God give us Luke chapter 3 clarity in the next epoch of American Church history—one that not only builds God's eternal kingdom and best fulfills the Great Commission, but best thwarts societal deterioration at the same time. The aforementioned ensuing benefits from reaching public servants for Christ are clear from Scripture.

Another essential aspect relative to what the Bible says is the key ingredient for a sustainable, successful nation will now be examined. I believe you will see how the missional priority of reaching public servants for Christ is indispensable to what follows.

PART III

*RIGHTEOUSNESS
EXALTS A NATION*

In the book of Proverbs, Solomon is addressing his son Rehoboam who would become the next political leader of Israel. Accordingly, under the inspiration of the Holy Spirit, Solomon is attempting to write the most pertinent wisdom—timeless principles on leadership, in fact—on how to manage and lead a nation.

Among the many lessons Solomon communicates is the need for personal righteousness—both in citizens *and* leaders, which is the single-most important asset any country can possess! This virtue, states Solomon, is preeminent to everything else because, as he pens in Proverbs 14:34,

Righteousness exalts a nation, but sin is a disgrace to any people.

First Kings 4:30 recounts that King Solomon, the wisest man to ever live, possessed unsurpassed wisdom. In Proverbs chapter 14, he proclaims that personal *righteousness* is an individual's most important asset and should be his primary focus in order for a nation to advance and thrive. Personal righteousness is what *exalts a nation*.

Solomon does not say that the presence of abundant natural resources or the excellence of its education system exalts a nation, as important as those two of many other examples are. Rather, he succinctly declares that personal *righteousness* exalts a nation (Proverbs 14:34)! When you consider his assertion, all hinges on the integrity and honesty of a nation's leaders and its citizenry.

Note by comparison republic/democracy-based countries where personal righteousness is absent, corruption exists, and what that absence does to that nation.[1] Republics and democracies are only as commendable as the people who administer them. Wise William Penn, again, said it this way:

> Governments, like clocks, go from the motion men give them, and as governments are made and moved by men, so by them

they are ruined also. Therefore governments depend upon men rather than men upon governments.[2]

This basic truth of dependence is often overlooked. Wouldn't it be interesting if a "National Righteous Meter" could somehow be compiled and published daily in the newspapers, much like the president's favorability numbers, sports league standings, the stock market, employment statistics, or the gross national product? Such a standard would serve to help us to best measure our national advancement or lack thereof, biblically speaking.

Accordingly, the manufacturing of righteous leaders is essential, but, in this sense, the institution of the State is like a mule: it cannot produce what it most desperately needs in order for it to survive as an entity. The State is dependent on the Church to do that task for them—whether or not the need is acknowledged. *Therefore, if the Church is slack in this regard or takes on other priorities, the State will soon suffer immeasurably for the lack of righteousness in its leaders.*

Because the preeminent and essential need for a nation is to have righteous leaders, this third part of *All in Authority* is written to underscore and persuade via yet another vein of biblical truth the fact that the institutional Church must be committed to discipling political leaders. As the Church goes, so goes the State. Said another way, as it pertains to this matter, the Church is causal, and the State is reflective.

Chapter 13

The Necessity of Righteousness

The Greek word for *righteousness* (*dikaiosune*) is used 86 times in the New Testament. The simplest and easiest way to remember the definition of this word is to divide the word: "right-way-ness." Worth underscoring, a careful observation of Proverbs 14:34 reveals a close tie between *righteousness* and *exaltation*; herein exists a cause-and-effect relationship. Great political leaders, great church leaders, great employers, great parents, and great husbands are always characterized by the biblical characteristics of *righteousness*. Their "right-way-ness" is what makes them effective leaders for the good of those whom they serve.

From a heavenly perspective, when a leader lives in alignment with God's character, he places himself in a position to be blessed by God. On the other hand, unrighteous leaders are never in a place or a position wherein God can extend them His grace and divine favor in as large a proportion.

The previous paragraph is worth repeating for emphasis and to persuade believers to be about discipling political leaders: *A nation's* *proportion of blessing is directly related to and tantamount to the **righteousness** quotient of its leaders.* Only when a nation is blessed with honorable, principled individuals does it place itself in a position to gain God's bestowal of blessing, favor, and overall well-being. All else stems from this "right-way-ness"!

> **The long-term exaltation of a nation is intrinsically intertwined with the righteousness of its leaders.**

Given this cut-to-the-chase analysis of a nation's greatest need, the question quickly becomes one of how *righteousness* is best formed in the life of its leaders.

No doubt you can see where I am going. As stated repeatedly in different ways in the preceding Part I and II, the critical, foremost duty of all believers is to witness for Christ and lead others to Him. In essence, every believer is to be about winning souls for Christ and especially the souls of the nation's political leaders.

In developing all that Solomon has to say about this matter of *righteousness*, it is the conversion of the soul and the ensuing discipleship of the individual, not moral foisting that is the only way to produce lasting, *righteous* individuals. When a person comes to Christ, he is indwelt by the Holy Spirit Who empowers a person to live *righteously*. Therefore, in our composite nation (one composed of both Church and State but institutionally separated[3]) the State is dependent on believers to diligently evangelize and disciple the unregenerate citizenry. The degree to which believers are faithful evangelizers and disciplers is directly proportional in the long term to the health and well-being of the State.

Lest you think Proverbs 14:34 stands alone exclaiming this profound truth, the following additional powerful passages in Proverbs serve to profoundly underscore and bolster this critically important axiom.

When it goes well with the righteous, the city rejoices,
And when the wicked perish, there is joyful shouting.
By the blessing of the upright a city is exalted,
But by the mouth of the wicked it is torn down (11:10–11).

When the righteous triumph, there is great glory,
But when the wicked rise, men hide themselves (28:12).

When the righteous increase, the people rejoice,
But when a wicked man rules, people groan (29:2).

These verses contain Solomon's repeated instructions to the nation's next political leader regarding, in essence, the relationship of repentance and conversion to the destiny of a country. As previously evidenced in Proverbs 14:34 and these passages, the following can be summarily concluded:

> The book of Proverbs repeatedly cries out about the relationship between the existence of righteous governmental leaders and the overall health of a city or a nation!

Again and again, this simple but profoundly important connection is woefully underemphasized in our increasingly secular culture—as if character no longer matters to the course of a nation! Furthermore, the previous Proverbs passages are not about the heavenlies; their pronounced principles relate to the here and now!

Chapter 14

The Progenitor of Righteousness

The necessity for the people of God to birth and develop righteous individuals in order to achieve an ongoing, healthy, *exalted nation* is explicitly articulated in Proverbs 11:30. Notice the direct connection:

The fruit of the righteous is a tree of life,
And he who is wise wins souls.

In beautifully descriptive Solomonic prose, the picture of *a tree of life* serves to illustrate the far-reaching effects of *the fruit of the righteous.* This *fruit* generally includes a person's influence, productivity, instruction, example, and progeny. Herein is a proverbial form used by Solomon wherein the second stanza informs the first stanza. Accordingly, notice specifically what is the causal agent of this *fruit*: the *winning of souls*!

This verse is yet another biblically exclamatory underscoring of the integral relationship between the importance of evangelism, which again results in the Holy Spirit's indwelling an individual. Elsewhere in Scripture, the Holy Spirit is deemed *the Helper* (cf. John 14:26) Who then aids in the achievement of inner and outward manifestations of *righteousness* in an individual.

With a genuine conversion and the indwelling *Helper*, it follows that we therefore *"seek first His kingdom and His righteousness"* (Matthew 6:33), and we become an evergreen *tree of life* in the lives of political leaders in any given nation!

States Charles Bridges, the author of one of the foremost commentaries on the book of Proverbs, in regard to the absence of soul winning:

> The Christian who neglects his brother's salvation, fearfully hazards [weakens] his own. He is gone back to his native selfishness, if he does not exhibit that "love and kindness of God that has appeared unto men"…How poor is the mitre [head dressing] or the crown; how debasing the wisdom of the philosopher, the scholar, or the statesman, compared with this wisdom![4]

The most important, wisest use of our time and resources as members of the Church universal is that of winning the lost, i.e., creating by the imputation of the Holy Spirit men and women who will *"hunger and thirst for righteousness"* their whole lives (cf. Matthew. 5:6). Summarily:

> It is the winning of souls that best fosters righteousness in a nation.

How misguided and biblically uninformed is the thinking and approach to the State of those who do not prioritize evangelism and discipleship—God's means of creating *righteous* individuals! Rarely is that formula postulated as the solution to America's downward moral trajectory, her economic woes, her increasing insecurity among other rival nations, and so forth.

Have we believers not come to grips with the profundity of these passages? Do we simply not believe them? Perhaps this ignorance is attributable to the famine of biblical literacy both in the nation as a whole and in the federal and state capitols? If indeed it is *righteousness that exalts a nation*, is not the priority of evangelism the key to a great country more so than any other achievement you might spend your time attempting to accomplish? What could be a more important priority than soul winning—and specifically winning the souls of present and future political leaders?

Stemming from the conversion of the soul and regeneration in Christ, Solomon explicitly states that five characteristics of *righteous* leadership can take root and produce long-lasting effects. Further unpacking the book of Proverbs relative to this subject reveals specific definitive aspects of *righteousness* that serve to exalt a nation via these most important characteristics in its leaders.

Chapter 15

Five Defining Characteristics of Righteousness

How do you specifically define what *righteousness* looks like? What are characteristic manifestations of its presence in a statesman? This chapter presents an organization of nearly all of the various passages from Proverbs that pertain to *righteousness* and define what *righteous* leadership must specifically embody. Therefore, a believer should emphasize the following five key areas when discipling a political leader.[5] In order to ***exalt a nation***, Solomon is saying a leader must possess the following characteristics of ***righteousness*** in the fullest measure:

A RIGHTEOUS LEADER MUST KNOW HE IS CALLED TO SERVE

In Proverbs 16:12, Solomon provides insights to Rehoboam as to what will establish and secure his future reign, i.e., his position of leadership:

> *It is an abomination for kings to commit wicked acts,*
> *For a throne is established on righteousness.*

The heart of public servants must hold a personal regard for those whom they serve as being more important than themselves (cf. Philippians 2:3). God requires that leaders whom He appoints to govern a country, His ordained institution of the State (cf. Romans 13:1), be a blessing to the people they serve.

In the eighth chapter of Ecclesiastes, a book also penned by Solomon, he specifically speaks to the degree of selflessness a leader must possess in his job:

> *A man has exercised authority over another man to his hurt* (v. 9b).

What a powerful way to express this concept! *A leader is to be so selfless that it hurts his own interests!*

Only from this biblical theology and the leader's ensuing knowledge, understanding, and submission to it can he possibly possess the realization that God has called him to office to serve in this way and to this degree. Leadership must cost him something; it must mean personal sacrifice! Only then can selfish motives possibly be eradicated and replaced by the ***righteous*** motives of selfless service commanded in and by the Word of God!

If a leader is secure and settled in the fact that God called him to serve in office, i.e., **He puts down one and exalts another** (Psalm 75:7b), then and only then is there no temptation to engineer his destiny; then and only then is there no temptation to perform the *wicked acts* often associated with self-preservation and/or advancement. In the aforementioned passages, *the theological construct in the inner heart* of the leader successfully and repeatedly fights off corruption.

Be sure of this:

> Abominable, wicked acts—corruption—grow in the unstable soil of self-preservation and/or visions of grandeur. The settled soil of "God placed me here to serve" nurtures a totally different variety of leader.

The DNA of the latter is this: "I understand my calling, and I am secure in it because I know God put me here for a season for the betterment of others." In essence then, believing that "God placed me here" is the belief that leads in part to *a throne ... established on righteousness* (Proverbs 16:12).

The believer who disciples a public servant must teach him these truths, namely: "Mr. Political Leader, if you want to establish yourself in office, then live securely according to a proper theologically based understanding of your calling. If you are self-centered, you will become less *established* due to your ensuing and inevitable *unrighteousness*."

The relationship between *righteousness* and being *established* parallels the previously seen relationship between *righteousness* and *exaltation*. *Righteous* character and behavior lead to both being *established* and being *exalted*—both individually and in a national sense.

In summary, *righteous* behavior in part stems from a public servant's knowing his or her calling in Christ and recognizing that God appointed him or her to office. It is up to God to preserve this public servant in office. Behaving *wickedly*, however, will stem from political leaders' believing they gained office through their own efforts. Such a premise leads to thinking they must be self-preserving.

A RIGHTEOUS LEADER MUST BE JUST

A major responsibility of civil government involves *the punishment of evildoers* (1 Peter 2:13–14). Romans 13:4 echoes this biblical understanding and perspective as to why God established this institution: *It does not bear the sword for nothing* states the Apostle Paul in that parallel passage. Within that realm of responsibility is the public servant's dispatch of just treatment through due process. A major responsibility of every elected official then is to make sure the city, county, state, and nation possess an excellent judicial system, especially God-fearing, *righteous* judges and police officers. Proverbs 20:8 states that this goal must be another priority of a believer's discipleship agenda.

> *A king who sits on the throne of justice*
> *Disperses all evil with his eyes.*

From the time of Moses, the leaders of Israel wore many distinct hats. When kings were also judges, as in the time of Solomon and Rehoboam, they would decree justice from their throne. They were to rule in fear of God. So it should be today in a nation's lawmaking, enforcement, and adjudication. Proverbs 24:23–25 states the following in this regard:

> *These also are sayings of the wise. To show partiality in judgment is not good. He who says to the wicked, "You are righteous," peoples will curse him, nations will abhor him; but to those who*

rebuke the wicked will be delight, and a good blessing will come upon them.

So great should be a ruler's judicial righteousness that he governs with total social and economic impartiality. Proverbs 31:8–9 states:

Open your mouth for the mute,
For the rights of all the unfortunate.

Open your mouth, judge righteously,
And defend the rights of the afflicted and needy.

Only through *righteous* lawmakers, enforcers, and courts can a State have any semblance of justice. Most certainly, *judging righteously* stems from *righteous* leaders. But how are those *righteous* leaders created, raised, and groomed? How does the State gain noble leaders?

Again, in God's design, they are to be manufactured by the institution of the Church. At the risk of sounding overly redundant, God-fearing individuals are created, raised, and equipped by the discipleship priorities of believers in a composite nation wherein exist the co-abiding institutions of Church and State. Wise is the State that upholds religious freedom so as to provide the Church ease in manufacturing *what the state most desperately requires*—the next generation of *righteous* State leaders. Keep in mind again that the State is not tooled by God to create what it most requires for its very survival—in this case, *righteous, just* leaders.

In summary, the second of the five characteristics of *righteousness* is *justice*. A government leader should be comfortable being a servant (the first of the five characteristics) and secondly committed to being *just* for such *exalts a nation*.

A RIGHTEOUS LEADER MUST BE DISCERNING

If *righteousness exalts a nation*, then it follows that good discernment by a public servant—in this case, most specifically, to associate with people of integrity—is a sure path to personal and ostensibly to national prosperity. To do otherwise is to be unduly and continually tempted by evil. *"Bad company corrupts good morals"* candidly states Paul in 1 Corinthians 15:33b. In other words, like begets like. Through discipleship, a Christian public servant would come to understand the following reality:

> Too often non-discerning elected officials associate with or hire people who do not represent their values.

As a believer discipling a political leader, make sure you underscore his or her need for discernment when hiring others. Staff must represent their boss's values in order to be effective in the long run. I am not saying to hire only Christians and fire non-Christians. (Such a belief is to endorse or at least begin to go down the road toward a theocratic form of government—a Church-controlled State, which the New Testament does not support.) In their spiritual immaturity, believers sometimes exhibit many more character flaws than do some nonbelievers and must be dismissed. And sometimes nonbelievers live according to God's principles—even though they fail to give attribution to the Author of those principles—and should be hired. The overarching point is this: disciple the public servant to be discerning as to whether the team he is building adequately represents his values.

In Proverbs 25:5, Solomon (in the context of training his son) summarily addresses this particularly important, timeless principle:

> *Take away the wicked before the king,*
> *And his throne will be established in righteousness.*

Hiring staff members is a critically important matter of utmost discernment as these choices will shape the political leaders' future to a great degree.

Furthermore, and very importantly, one specific form of ***wicked***[ness] ***before the king***, i.e., personal bribery, is highlighted several chapters later by Solomon. Bribery can undermine the best of legal and constitutional constructs, and there is virtually no way for a nation to manage the bribery of public officials, apart from the preceeding character development of the officeholder. This facilitation is due in large part to the fact that private, wire-transferable, non-investigable bank accounts are possible today in countries like Switzerland, Belize, and Malta. The only way to manage against such private corruption is through conviction against such malfeasance in the heart of those who would otherwise accept bribes. (Keep in mind, bribery is not a problem with people who have no power, but it is with those who do).

Samuel's sons took bribes, which ruined Israel. Bribes can ruin the best of republics and democracies. States Solomon in Proverbs 29:4 in this regard:

> *The king gives stability to the land by justice,*
> *But a man who takes bribes overthrows it.*

The wise statesman has been discipled by the believer to report incidences of bribery. His discipler taught him Numbers 32:23b, which says, ***and be sure your sin will find you out***.

In summary, the third of the five characteristics of ***righteousness*** is a believer's ability to be discerning and circumspect relative to the influence of others. Are you, as a believer, teaching the political leader to be first a servant; second, one who is just; and third, one who is discerning? Possessing such characteristics *exalts a nation*.

A RIGHTEOUS LEADER MUST HAVE CONVICTIONS

Whereas having convictions means more than having a knowledge of scriptural truths, convictions are certainly nothing less. Only by characteristic deliberateness and courageousness can knowledge become a conviction.

> *Like a trampled spring and a polluted well,*
> *Is a righteous man who gives way before the wicked*
> (Proverbs 25:26).

To lack conviction as a believer is often an indication of biblical illiteracy—if not an absence of courage.

In my decades of ministry to political leaders, I have seen a personal and direct correlation between those who shy away from in-depth Bible study and those who later fold under pressure.

For an elected Christian official to fall from his principles, i.e., to compromise biblical absolutes in his policies or interactions with others, grievously tarnishes the person's testimony and, I might add, the corporate testimony of the body of Christ. A person forms convictions by constant Bible study, prayer, meditation, and fellowship with other like-minded believers. Not to be underemphasized is the truth that convictions are either emboldened or weakened in relationship to weekly Bible study, prayer and meals with other believers.

In summary, the fourth of the five characteristics of *righteousness* is conviction. The Church must equip its men and women in public service to be servants, just, discerning, and in possession of inalterable convictions based on God's Word. Such *exalts a nation.*

A RIGHTEOUS LEADER IS PRAYERFUL

The last of the five characteristics of *righteousness* found in Proverbs is that of being *prayerful*. A believer who disciples a political leader must teach him to be prayerful. Note Proverbs 15:8–9 in this regard:

> *The sacrifice of the wicked is an abomination to the LORD,*
> *But the prayer of the upright is His delight.*
> *The way of the wicked is an abomination to the LORD,*
> *But He loves one who pursues righteousness.*

In these two back-to-back Proverbs of parallelism, *prayer* is equated with *righteousness* (the analogy follows the conjunction *"but"* in both passages). What every country most needs are men and women who have been taught by the Church to continually beseech and depend on God's guidance in their personal and State affairs. Furthermore, and particularly important to understand about this need, is the following:

> **The Bible says God only hears the prayers of leaders and citizens who are upright and righteous from His perspective, which means they have placed their faith in Jesus Christ.**

The Scripture is clear that the prayers of those who are at odds with God and who passively or actively reject the Son of God go unheard (other than the prayer of repentance). Preaching this truth is unpopular today as it is an inconvenient truth for those who are in the institution of the State to herald. Scripture, however, is replete and consistent on this matter, i.e., this truth is one that the institution of the Church must proclaim (with no fear of losing the next election).

Note the following passages in this regard:

The LORD is far from the wicked,
But He hears the prayer of the righteous (Proverbs 15:29).

"We know that God does not hear sinners; but if anyone is God-fearing and does His will, He hears him" (John 9:31).

If I regard wickedness in my heart,
The LORD will not hear;
But certainly God has heard;
He has given heed to the voice of my prayer.
Blessed be God,
Who has not turned away my prayer
Nor His lovingkindness from me (Psalm 66:18–20).

He who turns away his ear from listening to the law,
Even his prayer is an abomination (Proverbs 28:9).

But your iniquities have made a separation between you and your God,
And your sins have hidden His face from you so that He does not hear (Isaiah 59:2).

Public servants must be won to Christ for them to be effectively prayerful. The disciplemakers must be keenly aware of this fact when ministering to public officials.

In summary, the fifth of the five characteristics of *righteousness* is *prayerfulness.* As a believer, a pastor, or as the local church, are you teaching civil leaders to be a servant, to be just and discerning, to be conviction-driven and prayerful? Such exalts a nation.

SUMMARY

How utterly amazing it is that far too often personal *righteousness* is overlooked as an essential, preeminent ingredient to the dispatch of good civil government, the foundation of a healthy, prosperous nation. But how to produce such high-quality individuals to lead in the State is far more difficult than the simple analysis of the need. The only sure-based means to produce these virtues in leaders is through the evangelism and discipleship efforts of believers in the lives of those individuals. As the discipleship priorities, responsibilities, and manifestations of the Church go, so goes the State. Stated in another way:

> The State reflects the collective
> *righteousness* of its people—
> much more than it is the cause of it.

This succinct observation explains why so many republics and democracies with few or no disciple-making churches suffer. It stands to reason that the heralders of God's truth are critically important to the success of the public servant and the future of the country. The expositor/instructor of God's precepts is the seminal incubator of a country's present and future culture. In Hosea 4:6,

God summarily underscores this principle when He said to His Bible teachers of the time:

> *My people are destroyed for lack of knowledge.*
> *Because you have rejected knowledge,*
> *I also will reject you from being My priest.*
> *Since you have forgotten the law of your God,*
> *I also will forget your children.*

This OT passage, which explains the responsibility of Israel's priests to the nation's citizens, serves to reveal by way of applying its stated principle truth, the God-intended relationship between the Church and the State today. The timeless principle from Hosea, heralded through the ages, is this: *for the Church to fail to teach God's precepts to the leaders of the State is a sore subject in the eyes of God!* It is incumbent on the Church to teach God's precepts and manufacture citizens and righteous leaders in and for the State. Again, remember, the State is not in the business of creating its own effective leaders; therefore (even though she will not necessarily acknowledge it), the State must depend on the Church to do this for her.

These insights and the emphases of Proverbs regarding the seminal aspects pertaining to the health of a State clearly reveal the need for the continual development of *righteous* leadership. Definitively, a Solomonic spectral analysis of *righteousness* reveals at least five beautiful colors that every disciplemaker must teach to a political leader: service, justice, discernment, conviction, and prayerfulness. Such lead to the *exaltation* of a country!

Does your life model the very characteristics that Scripture reveals you must teach them? To the degree it does and to the degree you teach political leaders these truths is the degree to which you are the most strategically involved and at your best in the *exaltation* [of a] *nation*. Who in your church is an up-and-coming public servant that you should begin discipling today?

The missional priority of reaching public servants for Christ takes on yet another heightened dimension of importance when considering that God holds political leaders just as much responsible for the direction of the nation as He does Church leaders. That evidence will be explored in the next part.

PART IV

***WHOM DOES GOD
HOLD RESPONSIBLE FOR
THE DIRECTION OF A NATION?***

From the Old Testament to the New, the Bible is replete with examples regarding the priority and importance God places on reaching *kings and all who are in authority* with His Word (1 Timothy 2:2). The exegetical basis of this study, as discussed in Part I, indicates the Church is to focus on its calling to evangelize and disciple political leaders so that the Great Commission can be more efficiently and effectively fulfilled, through which simultaneously the righteousness in a nation can likewise be accomplished, preserved, and illuminated.

The second part examined how the Church has bungled her divine calling throughout history—not only to political leaders in specificity, but in general to the nation as a whole. Part III added yet another simple deduction: if righteousness is what exalts a nation, then the Church should be about the primacy of manufacturing righteous leaders for the nation.

Exploring this concept a step further requires examining more specifically how godly leaders impact nations. While each individual is accountable to God for his sins, whom, biblically, does God hold most responsible for the righteousness or the failings of a nation? The answer is its leaders. It follows that their leadership affects everyone else. Therefore, these are the men and women whom the body of Christ must prioritize relative to its equipping responsibilities as per Ephesians 4:11–12:

> *And He gave some as apostles, and some as prophets, and some as evangelists, and some as pastors and teachers, for the equipping of the saints for the work of service, to the building up of the body of Christ....*

Too often and too easily the decisions made by public servants are criticized, but give this conundrum some serious consideration:

> How can we expect those who do not know
> the Author of Scripture to write policies
> and laws in keeping with His precepts?

Are not Church leaders who fail to equip political leaders for office in part to blame? Who are we to complain if we have not done our part? Who will herald God's truths of new life in Christ if not His believers? Romans 10:14–15 further underscores this thought:

> **How then will they call on Him in whom they have not believed? How will they believe in Him whom they have not heard? And how will they hear without a preacher? How will they preach unless they are sent? Just as it is written, "HOW BEAUTIFUL ARE THE FEET OF THOSE WHO BRING GOOD NEWS OF GOOD THINGS!"**

These truths penned by the Apostle Paul in Ephesians chapter 4 and Romans chapter 10 become all the more sobering after peering for only seconds into the tiny two-chapter Old Testament book of Haggai. This book reveals an enormously insightful perspective and analysis, i.e., God's heavenly, transcendent perspective as to whom He holds ultimately responsible for the direction of a nation.

The prophet Haggai more than suggests that the underlying problem in any deteriorating nation is a spiritual one. Additionally, the spiritual problem starts with the leadership of a nation—both the leaders in the institution of the Church and the institution of the State.

I believe an overview providing some insights from this small but immensely powerful OT book in this specific regard will prove both compelling and informative in terms of personal missional emphasis and conviction. Israel had been an extraordinarily strong nation under the rules of King David and his son King Solomon. However, even during their reigns, the people stopped obeying God and afterward became increasingly disobedient. Consequently, the nation suffered great decline.

This deterioration should have come as no surprise to anyone, especially the Israelites, given the "if/then" structure of the Abrahamic Covenant found in the Torah, Genesis chapters 15 and 17, and fleshed out even more so in Deuteronomy chapter 28. That covenant said if God's chosen people obeyed God, He would prosper them, but if they disobeyed Him, He would chastise them (cf. Joshua 1 and Psalm 1). Their disobedience is evidenced by the many times God had warned them to cease from idolatry or be disciplined (cf. Hebrews 12:5–11).[1]

Under the subsequent reign of Solomon's son Rehoboam, the nation split into two entities: Israel and Judah. Regarding that division, keep in mind the book of Haggai focuses on the kingdom of Judah.[2] Like the noncompliant Northern Kingdom of Israel, Judah did not repent. After years of patience, God orchestrated the pagan nation of Babylon to be His surrogate of discipline and punishment. Under the leadership of King Nebuchadnezzar, the Babylonians sacked Judah, destroyed Solomon's Temple, and seized her people, carrying them into captivity.

Seventy years later, Babylon was sacked by a new world ruler, namely Persia. By God's design, under the direction of King Cyrus of Persia, the Jews were then permitted to return to their homeland and rebuild it. God, in His sovereignty and tough love, had orchestrated the sobering and humiliating conquest of His chosen people. He was at work through the pagan kings and their successors with the specific intent to wake up His people for His purposes.

Not much is known about the prophet Haggai other than the five prophesies recorded in this small book bearing his name. Haggai is the thirty-seventh of the thirty-nine OT books. The name *Haggai* means "festal one." Perhaps he was born on a feast day. Of further insight and interest is Haggai 2:3a, which states, ***"Who*** [else] ***is left*** *among you who saw the temple in its former glory?"* signifying that perhaps Haggai was over 70 years old (the time of the beginning of the Babylonian/Persian captivity) and had seen Solomon's Temple before its destruction.[3]

The OT book of Ezra mentions Haggai twice (cf. Ezra 5:1; 6:14) in tandem with the prophet Zechariah, whose book (also named after him) follows Haggai. The two-chapter long book of Haggai is the second shortest book in the OT after the one-chapter book of Obadiah. The book of Ezra provides an *overall* historical account of postexilic Judah, while Haggai's contribution is one of *spiritual* insight: an accounting during the same time period with a different emphasis.

The book of Haggai can be outlined around the five separate prophecies of Haggai. Of special note relative to the thesis of *All in Authority* is the first prophecy, but a sweeping overview of the book is helpful to understand before specifically studying the prophecies God used Haggai to record.

Chapter 16

Haggai's Five Prophecies

1. God's Rebuke of the Two Leaders—Haggai 1:2–11
2. God's Reinforcement of the Remnant—Haggai 1:13
3. God's Revelation to His People—Haggai 2:1–9
4. God's Reminder of the Past—Haggai 2:10–19
5. God's Reinstatement of the Davidic Lineage—Haggai 2:20–23

THE RETURN OF JUDAH

After the people had been held in captivity for 70 years, the Jewish civil leader Zerubbabel led 50,000 of the Judeans back to Jerusalem in the first of three waves of returnees. Since Zerubbabel was the political leader of the first wave, his life will be the one from whom parallels will be drawn. Joshua (or Jeshua as he is called in the book of Ezra) was the accompanying priest, and Haggai, of course, was the prophet.

Later Ezra and then Nehemiah would return with more people from Persia. Think of the three—Zerubbabel, Ezra, and

Nehemiah—as representing a later collective of Moses, in that Moses brought God's people out of Egyptian captivity into the Promised Land (cf. the book of Exodus). These three performed the same leadership roles at a later time in the life of Judah. Each of them faced the same postexilic problems:

- To build/rebuild their capital city
- To reinstitute Torah-based laws
- To overcome foreign enemies
- To purify the people from idolatry

Ezra, as mentioned in the book bearing his name, returned in the second wave—after the accounts in Haggai. To his deep dismay, he discovered that after seventy years of punishment, Judah had *once again so quickly* fallen into the same egregious sins of their forefathers! Skipping ahead, note Ezra's remedy to the deterioration of the nation in contrast to the present priest Joshua (who accompanied Haggai with the first returnees) in Ezra chapter 7.

> ***For Ezra had set his heart to study the law of the LORD and to practice it, and to teach His statutes and ordinances in Israel*** (Ezra 7:10).

The contrast between God's chastising Joshua for not making His directives a priority and Ezra's personal enterprise in taking the initiative to teach the Word of God foreshadows the point to be made in this part of *All in Authority*. This lesson in contrast is applicable to the deterioration of America or, for that matter, any nation. God expects His mouthpieces to proclaim the whole counsel of God (cf. Matthew 28:20; Acts 20:27)!

What can be learned from this short book of 38 verses as to whom God holds ultimately responsible for the direction of a nation?

Soon after Zerubbabel, the civic leader, and the 50,000 returned from Persia to Jerusalem, the local residents became upset with the Judeans' temple-rebuilding efforts. The flak from the locals speedily proved effective, and the newly returned-from-exile Judeans soon "spiritualized" the reason they had stopped rebuilding God's temple.

Note Haggai 1:2b, in which Haggai parrots the returnees' "spiritualized" procrastination and lack of courage with this excuse:

> *"The time has not come, even the time for the house of the L*ORD *to be rebuilt."*

Ironically, however, the people were very much about the business of building their own homes! The "time had come" for undertaking that particular endeavor! God was obviously not pleased with their choice. Sixteen years had now passed after their return, about 520 BC, and God delivered five prophecies via Haggai to once again remind the disobedient people of Judah that what was indeed presently happening in their lives was a result of their disobedience. But especially take note of God's disapproval.

HOLDING LEADERS ACCOUNTABLE

> God's rebuke was not aimed at the 50,000 returnees. Rather, God's rebuke was specifically directed toward Judah's civic and spiritual leaders.

This important distinction appears in the opening verse:

> *The word of the L*ORD *came by the prophet Haggai to Zerubbabel the son of Shealtiel, governor of Judah, and to Joshua the son of Jehozadak, the high priest, saying....*

Subsequent passages contain multiple uses of the pronoun *"you."*[4] To whom do these "yous" refer? *Of importance to the point being made in this part of this book: the "yous" relate only to those two individual leaders—Zerubbabel and Joshua.* Haggai's first admonitions centered only on the two who led His people and also named His name.

When examining the original Hebrew, the second person plural pronouns *"you"* are used throughout Haggai 1:1 to 1:12. Each instance is directly and only applicable to Zerubbabel and Joshua. Not until verse 12 does Haggai expand his remarks to include *all the remnant of the people.* In this instance and thereinafter, he uses the third person pronoun: *"their God."* In fact, many of the 12 "yous" in the NASB English translation of the original Hebrew text are supplied by the translation team for the sake of readability, but the point still stands that only the two leaders were initially held responsible for corporate Judah's possible judgment by God!

Again and importantly, God the Father, through His mouthpiece the prophet Haggai, first addresses His follower Zerubbabel, the civil leader of Judah, stating that the reason Judah was not being blessed was *the result of his and Joshua's spiritual lethargy*![5]

This insight should prove to be a driving force behind the strategy, formation, and missional manifestations of any and all believers and churches that are engaged in outreach. If God holds civil leaders responsible for the direction of a nation, as is the case in the book of Haggai, then should not the believer, the pastor, and the church prioritize evangelizing and discipling them? The answer is obviously and resoundingly YES!

Notice how God couches this directive in order to capture their attention in 1:5–6:

> *Now therefore, thus says the* LORD *of hosts, "Consider your ways! You* [Zerubbabel and Joshua] *have sown much, but harvest little; you eat, but there is not enough to be satisfied; you drink, but there is not enough to become drunk; you put on*

clothing, but no one is warm enough; and he who earns, earns wages to put into a purse with holes."

> Haggai's biting rebuke can be similarly applied to every civil and spiritual leader naming the name of Christ who procrastinates, outright ignores, or willfully disobeys the fulfilling of God's purposes.

This deficiency is the consequence and oft manifestation of civil leaders who have not been sufficiently discipled by the Church. Upon their return from Persian captivity, Judah, as a nation, made excuses as to why they couldn't devote more of their energies to God's work. Seemingly, Zerubbabel and Joshua were acquiescing to these excuses—if not positing them themselves. In essence, their seeming assent reveals their lack of fervor and conviction for the things of God, or their slippage is due to their failure in following the industrious and obedient-to-God "Ezra model," i.e., a strong, consistently present Bible teacher.

Judah, at least outwardly, journeyed to the nation's capital to reconstruct the Temple, but in reality, the people had lost their resolve and were now spending their time paneling their own homes and being lax about God's purposes.[6] Being self-deceived, they dragged their feet as they now made "spiritualized" excuses and phony defenses relative to communing with their God, working toward His purposes, and achieving them.

Note Haggai's specific rebuke in 1:4 in this regard:

"Is it time for you yourselves [Zerubbabel and Joshua] *to dwell in your paneled houses while this house lies desolate?"*

Because of their unfaithfulness to be about God's purposes, He Himself orchestrated the withholding of national blessing! In 1:11 God states the extent of His discipline:

"I called for a drought on the land, on the mountains, on the grain, on the new wine, on the oil, on what the ground produces, on men, on cattle, and on all the labor of your hands."

Should we not expect these same kinds of national sowing and reaping consequences due to civil leaders who name the name of Christ being spiritually immature, if not spiritually disobedient, because they have not been discipled by the Church? While there is no NT evidence of God's judging nations today through His abandonment wrath, the principle of sowing and reaping in the lives of individuals and nations runs throughout the Bible. Bad decisions by individual leaders result in bad consequences for corporate nations.

Chapter 17

A Profound Play on Words

In the original Hebrew text, the intentional play on words that God gives to Haggai is both interesting and noteworthy. In verse 4, the Hebrew word for **desolate** is *hareb*, and the word for **drought** in verse 11 is *horeb*. God is instructing Haggai to use words that were quite similar in order to unmistakably drive home His point! God wanted His wayward people to make the connection!

The **drought** in the land was because of their **desolation** (*desolate*—"to make bleakly, depressingly empty") of His temple! Their dismal attention to His business was now resulting in God's bleak attention to their matters! God was the One behind the overall decline of the nation! Why? Because the national leaders—the civil and spiritual leaders—had become self-serving![7]

The nation's leaders had returned from Persia with good motives, but the local residents' resistance to their dreams, coupled with the affairs of everyday life, began to crowd out their earnestness, convictions, and original intent. After 16 years they no longer had time, desire, nor inclination to serve God's purposes. Their selfish pursuits had turned to more "important" tasks.

Again, contrast this attitude with the priest/Bible teacher Ezra.[8] He had not returned from Persia at this point; but upon his arrival, he began to teach the Word of God. His teaching made the difference!

Joshua had seemingly become lax in his duties; and once again, Hosea 4:6 bluntly warns the nation about the seriousness of the priests' failure to do their job:

> *My people are destroyed for lack of knowledge.*
> *Because you have rejected knowledge,*
> *I also will reject you from being My priest.*
> *Since you have forgotten the law of your God,*
> *I also will forget your children.*

This passage appropriately and insightfully serves to diagnose the spiritual lethargy and possible consequences that had now beset the nation. The returnees hadn't made their personal spiritual vitality a priority!

This book also serves to vividly illustrate the principal truth of Matthew 6:33 in the New Testament: ***"Seek first His kingdom and His righteousness, and all these things will be added to you."***

> The returning multitudes of Judeans—
> and even their spiritual and civil
> leaders—were in desperate need of a
> Bible teacher who could mature and
> rekindle in them the ways of God!

Similarly, today when the leaders of the Church manifest themselves in ways more like Joshua than Ezra, the Zerubbabels of this world (the political leaders of a nation) will be less than what they would be if the Church had been intent on discipling them and teaching them the whole counsel of God! It follows that those believers who fail to disciple political leaders end up living in a country that is less than desirable—but the book of Haggai serves to indicate that their failure is their own fault.

Chapter 18

Insights from Sodom and Gomorrah vs. Postexilic Judah

The Scriptures establish that God withheld His *national* blessings on Judah—due to their leaders' personal spiritual sluggishness. This *causal* insight is quite interesting when compared to the actual reason God destroyed Sodom and Gomorrah in Genesis chapters 18 and 19. God was ready to reduce the cities to ashes because the debauchery of Sodom and Gomorrah was ***indeed great, and their sin is exceedingly grave*** (cf.18:20b.) But prior to Sodom and Gomorrah's destruction and especially important to the thesis of this part of *All in Authority*, note in verse 23 that Abraham inquired *"Will You* [God] *indeed sweep away the righteous with the wicked?"* Then God's friend began to negotiate, asking God if He would spare the cities if 50 righteous people were found.

God answered, *"I will spare the whole place on their account"* (18:26b).

Realizing that there probably weren't 50 righteous people, Abraham reduced the number to 45, and God agreed to spare the cities for that number. Abraham continued to bargain with God, lowering the number incrementally to only ten. Would He spare the cities for a mere ten people? God's patience is so generous. *"I will not destroy it on account of the ten,"* He replied (v. 18:32b).

Why am I mentioning this instance? Contrast this insight into the mind of God as revealed in Genesis 18 as it pertains to His determination of whether to judge a city or a nation with the insight provided from Haggai chapter 1. In Genesis 18, the biblical text evidences that God's enactment of judgment would not have been instituted if only a few of the multitudes had been found faithful in the cities! If only a few of the multitudes are faithful to Him, He will not judge the whole.

But in the book of Haggai, God's judgment was enacted on an entire city full of followers *when the leaders who named His name* were found to be spiritually lethargic! I believe this comparison is most insightful and profound! In principle, what does it mean?

WHAT MIGHT HAGGAI SAY TO MISSIONS-MINDED BELIEVERS TODAY?

Given this insight into God's way of thinking as it relates to His willingness to withhold the pouring out of His consequential judgment, I believe that Haggai would state the following to missions-minded believers today who name the name of Christ:

> God's blessing on your nation is primarily
> determined by the faithfulness of
> political and spiritual leaders whom

> God has put into office more so than the
> faithfulness of the multitudes.

The determination of whether God gives or withholds blessing a nation is not so much about the quantity of godly churches or individuals as it is the godliness of the leadership!

Genesis 18:28–33 reveals that God was willing to refrain from judging Sodom and Gomorrah if only 10 individuals found there had been faithful to Him! America has millions of faithful and committed Christians, as do other select nations in the world. Therefore, it stands to reason that the number of faithful believers is not the determining factor relative to God's invoking His consequential judgment. Rather, as evidenced in Haggai 1, the health of a nation is dependent much more so on the faithfulness of believers in office! What they sow the nation reaps!

> The book of Haggai serves to indicate that
> the health of a nation depends on the
> spiritual maturity, passion, action, and
> obedience to the special calling of political
> leaders who name the name of Christ.

Faithful leaders please God and bring about His blessings—something our nation is in dire need of![9]

So the obvious application and takeaway from the book of Haggai is as follows: with this principle in view, the Church must be actively involved in the State, evangelizing and discipling its civic leaders!

What are you doing as a believer—retired businessman, Bible teacher, pastor—to evangelize and disciple political leaders? Church, what are you doing to evangelize and disciple political leaders? Are you prioritizing reaching political leaders in your missional strategy because you realize the health and future of the nation is at hand? God expects you to know that, my friend.

OBEDIENT-TO-CHRIST LEADERS BENEFIT THE NATION

When the prophet Haggai reminded Zerubbabel, Joshua, and the multitudes who had taken up the challenge to return to the capital city of Jerusalem of their unfulfilled promise to rebuild God's temple, they responded appropriately.

> *Then Zerubbabel the son of Shealtiel,* [the civil leader] *and Joshua the son of Jehozadak, the high priest, with all the remnant of the people, obeyed the voice of the* Lord *their God and the words of Haggai the prophet, as the* Lord *their God had sent him. And the people showed reverence for the* Lord (1:12).

God's leaders and His people first looked inwardly at their own sin of materialism and selfishness (1:4) and repented. This poignant, sobering short narrative of Haggai 1 serves to underscore and parallel the timeless truths of 2 Chronicles 7:14 and 1 Peter 4:17, respectively:

> *"And My people who are called by My name humble themselves and pray and seek My face and turn from their wicked ways, then I will hear from heaven, will forgive their sin and will heal their land."*

> *For it is time for judgment to begin with the household of God; and if it begins with us first, what will be the outcome for those who do not obey the gospel of God?*

SUMMARY

This book has disclosed profound implications for those who are called to disciple civil leaders—the Church universal. The small OT book of Haggai provides a sobering, hugely insightful, godly perspective on why a nation experiences decline (cf. 2 Chronicles 7:14; 1 Peter 4:17) and, even more encouragingly, how that nation can be turned around to prosper.

Don't miss the fact that this book places the demise of a country squarely on the shoulders of the followers of Yahweh—most specifically on those whom He has placed in leadership of the Church and State.

A survey of Haggai would not be complete without noting the following additional passages (from an agrarian-based culture) that so depict and parallel America's enormous problems today.

> *"'From that time when one came to a grain heap of twenty measures, there would be only ten; and when one came to the wine vat to draw fifty measures, there would be only twenty. I smote you and every work of your hands with blasting wind, mildew and hail; yet you did not come back to Me,' declares the LORD.... 'Is the seed still in the barn? Even including the vine, the fig tree, the pomegranate and the olive tree, it has not borne fruit...'"* (Haggai 2:16–17, 19).

Again, God blamed the civil and spiritual leaders of Judah for the country's economic woes and overall decline. The responsibility was laid first on the shoulders of God's civil and spiritual leaders because they were not *seeking first the kingdom of God*. Rather, these leaders were seeking first the god of self-interest (cf. 1:4)!

> The Church's priority to evangelize and disciple political leaders has much to do with determining the course of a nation.

As Haggai saw it, the solution to his nation's woes was not a political matter; it was first a spiritual concern. What has always been most important to God is the spiritual temperature of a nation. What triggers God's gracious, transcendent blessing on a nation hinges on His believers' faithfulness to disciple individual political leaders—the long-term, real determining factor as to whether He blesses or disciplines the nation. Don't miss the certainty of this truth![10]

Will you disciple the next Zerubbabel who, when confronted, will *obey the voice of the LORD* (1:12)? The fascinating, short book of Haggai says that both spiritual (Joshua) and civil (Zerubbabel) leaders and their obedience (or lack thereof) to the Lord are the predominant issue in the destiny of a nation. Therefore, the Church should target political leaders above all others; they must be its missional priority for all the reasons stated!

Perhaps the best historical illustration of the thesis of this book is provided by the story of William Wilberforce and the pastor behind the scenes who equipped Wilberforce to achieve an awe-inspiring outcome that many in his time thought impossible. I think this example best encapsulates what has been advocated in *All in Authority*, i.e., what God can do when the Church accepts its divine calling and prioritizes evangelizing and discipling political leaders.

Wilberforce and John Newton pack all of these principles in human example.

PART V

WILBERFORCE: A MAN WHO "TURNED THE WORLD UPSIDE DOWN"

In the first century, a handful of ragtag disciples of Jesus Christ who held within their hearts the love of God and a passion for taking as many souls with them to heaven as possible *turned the world upside down*. Filled with the Holy Spirit after Christ's ascension, these committed, dedicated, determined, and undaunted disciples fearlessly followed the command of our Lord to spread His Word of repentance and redemption not only to the multitudes, but also and specifically to the influencers of their time—*kings and all who are in authority*.

In 1833 a British lawmaker stunned a watching world when he succeeded in his career-long fight to end slavery in Great Britain. Lesser known to the world is the man largely responsible for this achievement: Pastor John Newton, the resolute pillar who worked indefatigably behind the scenes discipling Wilberforce in the Word of God. Halting the business of buying and selling their fellowman impacted millions of people during their time and long into the future.

Britain transported an estimated 3.1 million Africans (of whom 2.7 million arrived) to the British colonies in the Caribbean, North and South America, and other countries.[1] Consider those who benefitted from the law halting such transport, the millions upon millions of men and women who, instead of being abducted, held captive in the bowels of a slave ship, and destined for heavy labor on some foreign shore, were able to live out their days in their own communities in the embrace of families and friends. Think of their descendants and what their contributions to the world may have been. Truly, Wilberforce and Newton *turned the world upside down* in their time and greatly impacted the future.

What about you in our time? What are the egregious issues that God calls us to stand against or the righteous ones He calls us to defend in this world more than at any time in recent history? What is our work to turn *the world upside down*?

May the pastor, the layman, the Bible school teacher, the person who senses a call from God to change the world one heart at a time also consider reaching political leaders for Christ. May the remarkable story of William Wilberforce and the humble pastor who discipled him to become a stalwart man of God who dared change the world serve as a backdrop to that end.

Chapter 19

What Motivated William Wilberforce?

British lawmaker William Wilberforce had tried and failed to persuade Parliament to abolish the slave trade for 20 years. Finally in 1807, Parliament passed the bill to abolish the use of British ships to transport captives for slavery, but not slavery itself. On July 26, 1833, after Wilberforce had left office and only three days before he died, Great Britain's House of Commons passed the Slavery Abolition Act and ended the practice of African slave trading throughout its empire.

What can today's believers learn from the example of Wilberforce, especially when it comes to the role of the Church in politics? William Wilberforce would most likely be a forgotten figure in history had it not been for John Newton, who remained singularly focused on his calling, which was making disciples of Jesus Christ by teaching the Word of God. He was perhaps correspondingly as responsible for ending the slave trade in Britain as Wilberforce, yet he never directly engaged in politics. Newton was pre-political.

The motion picture *Amazing Grace* highlights the life of William Wilberforce. The title is derived from the famous Christian hymn by the same name, written by Newton. A self-described "wretched man," Newton had been a slave trader before being dramatically saved by the powerful message of the gospel of Jesus Christ. After Newton's conversion, he became a pastor and had a profound personal impact on Wilberforce—not a *political* impact, but a *spiritual* one.

Newton and other ministers within the Church were responsible for helping Wilberforce develop convictions born from Scripture. Their discipleship efforts led Wilberforce to become a man driven by theology and doctrine.

The influence of the Church made Wilberforce who he was through the ministry of the Word.

After Wilberforce became a Christian, he decided to spend legislative recesses studying the Bible. Spending ten hours per day studying and memorizing Scripture was common for him. This righteous conviction rooted in biblical doctrine is what sustained and directed Wilberforce during his decades-long battle against the practice of slavery. Wilberforce's vital work occurred in the late 1700s. His life serves to illustrate well the thesis of this book.

One of the darkest chapters in American history is nineteenth-century African slavery. During America's Civil War (1861–1865), Bible scholars on both sides of the slavery issue were firing theological volleys back and forth at one another in one of two attempts:

1. to decry the enslavement of one human being by another or
2. to justify slavery by aligning it with slavery in the Bible.[2]

Commenting on this theological warfare, one historian writes the following:

Abolitionists argued vehemently that, based on the Bible, the spirit of Christianity forbids the enslavement of one race by another. Slavery's defenders in the South argued just as vehemently that the Bible itself did not condemn slavery but took it for granted.[3]

While my purpose is not to reconstruct and analyze the theological arguments surrounding this human atrocity, my firm conviction is that nineteenth-century African slavery in America was in no way biblically justified.[4] Nor was it justified in Great Britain.

We easily and correctly marvel at Wilberforce's great accomplishment.[5] But regarding the role of the Church, isn't the pertinent question the following: how did Wilberforce persevere in his multi-decadal quest that changed the course of a nation?

Contemporary Christian activists[6] often cite this man as the par excellence example of Christian political activism.[7] His ultimately successful near forty-year fight in British Parliament to end slavery is looked upon as a jewel in the crown of moralistic campaigning. While it cannot be denied that Wilberforce fought a persevering, meritorious fight, prevailing against the odds and helping to eradicate a vile cancer from his part of the world, what sustained him as he fought the good fight for so long? Was he motivated by the simple desire to take back the culture? Or was there something deeper that put the fire in his bones to fight for righteousness?

Wilberforce's life bears out the Word of God dwelling richly in him, a vibrant and growing faith in the Lord Jesus Christ that steered his political career, informed his convictions, and gave him the motivation to persevere against incredible odds.[8] Dear reader, this same God-given wisdom is available to every Christian legislator today who believes in Jesus Christ and submits himself/herself to the Word of God. In Wilberforce's own words:

The diligent perusal of the Holy Scriptures would discover to us our past ignorance. We should cease to be deceived by superficial appearances, and to confound the Gospel of Christ with the systems of philosophers; we should become impressed with that weighty truth, so much forgotten, and never to be too strongly insisted on, that Christianity calls on us, as we value our immortal souls, not merely in general, to be religious and moral, but specially to believe the doctrines, and imbibe the principles, and practice the precepts of Christ.[9]

In yet another way to answer what motivated him, Wilberforce was involved in Bible study with other believers in Parliament—a Bible study that was led by a skilled Bible teacher named John Newton.

It saddens my heart that so many believers in office in America today do not get this! How unfortunate it is for me, after decades of ministry in both the California and Washington, D.C. Capitols, to see believers leave office in discouragement. Is this despondency due in part to the fact that while in office, many of them never connected to a Bible study—or to their fellow Christian colleagues in that Bible study?

Chapter 20

Who Was Wilberforce?

William Wilberforce, a contemporary of some of England's (as well as history's) greatest preachers, including John Newton, John Wesley, and George Whitefield,[10] was born in 1759 in Hull, England. God used unusual circumstances in the life of young Wilberforce to bring him into the company of Evangelicals and one of these great men of God in particular, John Newton.[11]

Writes Wilberforce biographer John Pollock:

> [W]hen William was turning nine, his father died at the age of forty. Abel Smith became head of the business; the firm changed its name to Wilberforce and Smith, and William's life changed too. Not merely because he would be independent and quite rich when he came of age, but because he was sent, a year after his father's death, to live with his childless uncle and aunt, William and Hannah Wilberforce, at their Wimbledon villa in the Surrey countryside and their London house in St. James's Place. They put him to boarding school at Putney.[12]

As it turned out for young William,

> These relatives were despised Evangelicals, friends of the preacher George Whitefield, a leader in the first Great Awakening, and John Newton, best known today as the author of "Amazing Grace." Newton, an old seadog, ex-naval deserter, ex-lecher, and ex-slave-trader who had been converted slowly in and after a storm at sea, fascinated the boy with his yarns. And Newton showed little William "how sweet the name of Jesus sounds" until his mother, horrified that he was turning "Methodist," took him away.[13]

An article by Steven Gertz on Wilberforce's relationship with Newton states, "As a boy of eight years [or nine!], he [Wilberforce] sat at the feet of the fascinating sea-captain [Newton], drinking in his colorful stories, jokes, songs—and perhaps most importantly, lessons of faith."[14]

Later in life…

> William remembered a younger Evangelical, John Newton, the parson of Olney in Buckinghamshire who often preached in London and was soon to be famous as a hymn-writer. A boy could hardly fail to be impressed by this jolly, affectionate ex-sea captain and slaver, who as a youth had been flogged in the Royal Navy for desertion and later suffered as the virtual slave of a white man's native mistress in West Africa. Wilberforce listened enthralled to his sermons and his stories, even "reverencing him as a parent when I was a child."[15]

Seeds of faith may have been planted in young Wilberforce's life, yet the real fruit of true salvation was still years away. Wilberforce, Piper notes, "had admired George Whitefield, John Wesley, and John

Newton as a child. But soon he left all the influence of the evangelicals behind."[16]

As noted previously, Wilberforce's "mother was more high church and was concerned her son was 'turning Methodist.' So she took him out of the boarding school where they had sent him and put him in another."[17]

> In the holidays the Wilberforce family began to scrub William's soul clear of Wimbledon and Clapham a slow process: he [William] wrote manfully to his uncle [who he was pulled away from] of endurance under persecution [from his family], and of increasing "in the knowledge of God and Christ Jesus whom he sent, whom to know is life eternal."[18]

In Wilberforce's life, the intervening time between his childhood exposure to Newton and his later conversion via Isaac Milner's ministry was one of spiritual deadness. Says one writer about Wilberforce's college years, he "lost any interest in biblical religion and loved circulating among the social elite."[19] So far had he drifted, "Newton said sadly that nothing seemed left of his [Wilberforce's] faith except a more moral outlook than was usual among men of fashion."[20] Being moral, apart from regeneration, was no more salvific back then than it is now...or ever will be!

Chapter 21

Coming to Faith in Jesus Christ

In the spiritual vacuum of his heart, Wilberforce made room for the popular religion of his day.

> In London, he [Wilberforce] had a sitting at the Essex Street chapel founded by Theophilus Lindsey, the "father" of modern Unitarianism, one of the few clergy of the Church of England who had shown courage and principle enough to resign their livings on abandoning, like so many, a belief in the divinity of Jesus Christ. Lindsey still preached the Christian ethic and read the Church services, and his chapel attracted several eminent men: Wilberforce rated him London's only fervent preacher, since the Evangelical or "methodistical" preachers he had enjoyed with the uncle and aunt were now outside his pale.[21]

But Wilberforce would eventually be saved from this anti-biblical notion of Jesus Christ. This was Britain's equivalent to America's epoch of Theological Liberalism as described in Part II of this book.

Wilberforce's subsequent accounts of his long drawn out conversion or perhaps Rededication to the Christ of his boyhood faith—are somewhat contradictory but he gives a prime share to his reading Doddridge's book with Milner. They possibly looked up relevant passages in the Bible, for Wilberforce says he adopted his religious principles from the "perusal of the Holy Scriptures" and...the instruction I derived from a friend of very extraordinary natural and acquired powers.[22]

Wilberforce had come to salvation in Jesus Christ at age twenty-five,[23] a few years before a life-changing meeting with Newton. According to one biographical sketch of Wilberforce's life, after he won his election to Parliament in 1784, he "agreed to take a tour of the continent....When he happened to run into his old schoolmaster from Hull, Isaac Milner, Wilberforce impulsively invited him to join the traveling party. That invitation was to change Wilberforce's life."[24]

By the time Milner deposited him on 22 February 1785 at Number 10 Downing Street, Wilberforce had reached intellectual assent to the Biblical view of man, God and Christ. He thrust it to the back of his mind and resumed his social and political life.[25]

In the summer of that year, "slowly intellectual assent became profound conviction."[26] But still not a Christian by his own summation, it was not until "the third week of October 1785 the 'great change,' as he afterwards termed it, had driven Wilberforce to rise early each morning to pray."[27] The story goes that Milner spoke of his Christian faith to Wilberforce and that the latter "initially treated the subject flippantly, but eventually agreed to read the scriptures daily."[28]

Chapter 22

Wilberforce's Crisis of Faith

Faced with tremendous difficulty over how to reconcile his political career with his new life in Christ, a weary and confused[29] Wilberforce "turned to his boyhood hero, John Newton, now sixty years old and Rector of St. Mary Woolnoth in the City."[30]

Says Gertz of Wilberforce's 1785 meeting with Newton:

> Now, in a moment of spiritual crisis, wondering whether his reborn faith in God required him to leave politics, Wilberforce knew who could help him most...he mustered his courage and strode to the front door to call on his old friend.[31]

It is noteworthy that when it came to his political career, Wilberforce sought counsel from none other than a minister of the Word of God. Newton advised Wilberforce to stay in office and pursue Christ as well.

What can be learned from Newton and Wilberforce pertaining to the differing roles of Church and State?

Newton and Wilberforce serve to magnificently model a clear, biblically correct understanding as previously set forth in this book of the relationship between the institution of the Church and the institution of the State. *The former is to disciple the latter versus trying to do its job!*

By God's design, the Church is to be pre-political. God appointed Wilberforce to lead in His institution of the State, whereas God appointed Newton to lead in His institution of the Church. The former is called to moralize the unregenerate through law creation and enforcement; the latter is called to make disciples.

As mentioned in the preamble, for leaders in the Church to assume the work of God's leaders in the State is highly ineffective—especially while turning a blind eye to their call of making disciples of the State's leaders. This erroneous direction is akin to the Religious Right epoch in America church history as described in chapter 12 of this book.

Chapter 23

The Life of a Saved Politician

Once saved and sure that he should stay in politics, Wilberforce "worked hard to strengthen not only [his] mental but spiritual stamina."[32] In the process, the Bible became his most beloved book, and he sought to learn portions of the Word by heart.[33]

He memorized portions "so that he could meditate at night, or should his eyes trouble him, or when needing guidance in his place in the Commons or at committees."[34] In other words, he *Let the word of Christ richly dwell* in him (Colossians 3:16).

Perhaps most telling of the primacy of salvation over the entirety of his life is the following statement by Pollack:

> For Wilberforce wanted to subject not merely his appetites but his politics to Christ: "A man who acts from the principle I profess," he told a constituent three years after the conversion, "reflects that he is to give an account of his political conduct at the Judgment seat of Christ."[35]

Wilberforce's reliance on and accountability to biblical precepts underlie the tremendous actions and positions he took as a legislator—namely, fighting a nearly forty-year battle to abolish the African slave trade. It is unfortunate that the latter fact about Wilberforce is often trumpeted without a proper and necessary emphasis and understanding of the former. Likened to a faithful pastor-teacher who is continually mindful of James 3:1, ***Let not many of you become teachers, my brethren, knowing that as such we will incur a stricter judgment***, Wilberforce seemingly had similar sentiments about answering to the Lord Jesus Christ one day for his political endeavors as ***a minister of God...for good*** (Romans 13:4).

Only a few years after his conversion, Wilberforce began to set his heart slowly on abolishing the slave trade. Much could be said from a historical perspective about the providential workings of God through specific people and circumstances that brought the issue to a rolling boil in Wilberforce's heart, but suffice it to say that God raised up the right person at the right time for the right task.

Chapter 24

Wilberforce's "Two Great Objects"[36]

Slavery was rampant in Great Britain during Wilberforce's lifetime. The [slave] Trade was legalized by Royal Charters of 1631, 1633 and 1672 and by Act of Parliament in 1698. One of the most prized fruits of the War of Spanish Succession was the Assiento clause of the Treaty of Utrecht, giving Britain the sole right to supply slaves to the Spanish Colonies.[37]

In the years following his conversion to Jesus Christ, Wilberforce became convinced that God had called him through His Providence to specific tasks:

Wilberforce stated this mission in his diary entry on October 28, 1787, when he was a young twenty-eight-year-old parliamentarian. With the menacing black clouds of the French Revolution rolling up on the horizon and Britain's own social conditions providing cause for grave concern, he wrote simply: "God Almighty has set before me two great objects, the suppression of the Slave Trade and the reformation of manners."[38]

These convictions were what led him to tirelessly pursue the abolition of slavery for 20 years,[39] as well as societal reform. Author Charles Colson observes that during these years, Wilberforce came to an important conclusion concerning the second of his two aims:

> It was the great genius of Wilberforce that he realized that attempts at political reform without, at the same time, changing the hearts and minds of people were futile.[40]

Wilberforce's platform to reform the manners of Britain is worth mentioning due to the methodology he used to effect change. Writes John Pollock:

> Interestingly, the campaign was never specifically religious. Wilberforce never tried to enlist the religious or even the professedly moral. Some of the grandees whose support he gained were in fact notoriously dissolute. But Wilberforce believed strongly that the destinies of a nation could best be influenced by deeply committed followers of Christ, and that conversion to Christ was a person's most important political action as well as religious.[41]

Wilberforce's perspective on the public arena placed a premium on salvation and also emphasized the importance of understanding sound doctrine. Piper sheds valuable light on Wilberforce's biblical presuppositions:

What made Wilberforce tick was a profound biblical allegiance to what he called the "peculiar doctrines"[42] of Christianity. These, he said, give rise in turn to true "affections" for spiritual things, which then break the power of pride and greed and fear and lead to transformed morals, which lead to the political welfare of the nation. No true Christian can endure in battling unrighteousness unless his heart is aflame with new spiritual affections, or passions.[43]

By his placing such a premium on Christ and sound doctrine, is there any question about the epistemological basis from which Wilberforce operated? Wilberforce diagnosed the root cause of Britain's sliding moral condition as being connected with a low view of genuine Christian doctrine. Observing the attitude of his day, he commented,

> The fatal habit of considering Christian morals as distinct from Christian doctrines insensibly gained strength. Thus the "peculiar doctrines" of Christianity went more and more out of sight, and as might naturally have been expected, the moral system itself also began to wither and decay, being robbed of that which should have supplied it with life and nutriment.[44]

If Christian morals and Christian doctrines need to be connected as Wilberforce suggested, should not a country that desires a return to a God-honoring culture strive to reconnect them?

> The first step involves understanding and imbibing on those "peculiar doctrines" versus trying to change a nation's laws!

If Wilberforce was right, the latter flows out of the former, and he personified what he preached. He made the case for the evangelism, discipleship, and in-depth expositional teaching of God's Word to our governmental leaders both in principle and in historical example!

The fruit of his premises and personifications was discernible throughout British life well into the next century: "Whatever its faults, nineteenth-century British public life became famous for its emphasis on character, morals, and justice and the British business world famous for integrity."[45] What sweet relief to a country once ravaged by untold human suffering! Salvation in and the doctrines of Christ energized Wilberforce's political life and motivated him to reshape his culture![46]

Driven by sound biblical theology, Wilberforce did much for the morals of the culture—not only for the benefit of his day but also for the years that followed. As for his other "great objective":

> It was a full forty-six years later and only three days before his death on July 26, 1833, when the bill for the abolition of slavery throughout the entire British Empire passed its second reading in the House of Commons.[47]

Not only had Wilberforce succeeded in crippling the slave trade by outlawing British transport in 1807, but his efforts also shut down the entire insidious institution! A lifetime of work changed the world for the benefit of millions of people, but that favorable outcome all began first with a change in the heart of the man who would one day turn *the world upside down*. Wilberforce faithfully pursued his God-given mission with the help of his Church mentors.

Chapter 25

The Importance of Evangelism and Discipleship in Wilberforce's Life

> The back of the British slave trade was broken not by political activists, that is, not by Christians who attempt to change civil laws with no consideration for the hearts of legislators, but rather, by a man of God who stood on and for the truth of Scriptures.

As a lifelong member of Parliament who never lost an election,[48] Wilberforce made himself strong in the doctrines of grace[49] and allowed himself to be discipled by great men of the Church like Isaac Milner and John Newton.

It is important to note that Wilberforce was not strong in his own strength (1 Corinthians 1:27); rather, in his humility lay his strength.

In 1785, at the risk of ostracism, Wilberforce continually met with Newton, a man whom Parliament despised. Through these meetings and the sound teaching he received in both his childhood and adult years, Wilberforce grew bold in Christ. I have restated this fact because of how important it is to grasp the scope of influence John Newton had on Wilberforce.

Newton later said to Wilberforce, "It is hoped and believed that the Lord has raised you up for the good of His Church and for the good of the nation."[50] Keep in mind too that Wilberforce's relationship with Newton came about despite the counsel of his close colleague, Prime Minister William Pitt, who attempted to pressure him away from Newton.

Pitt soundly castigated Newton as an Evangelical who would render Wilberforce's talents useless both to himself and mankind. Nothing, as it turned out, could have been further from the truth!

Many legislators who read this book will have to, or have already had to, surmount the same counsel of their colleagues relative to attending my Bible studies for members. We must all keep in mind what the Apostle Paul stated in Galatians 1:10, *For am I now seeking the favor of men, or of God? Or am I striving to please men? If I were still trying to please men, I would not be a bond-servant of Christ.* Your answer and mine to Paul's question is critical. Will some end up sitting in the seat of scoffers or the counsel of the wise in Christ?[51]

Wilberforce did not shirk from the truth written on his heart by the Word of God through the power of the indwelling Holy Spirit. Writes Pollock:

> In planning moral reform he showed awareness that politics are influenced more by the climate of an age than by the personal piety of statesmen and politicians. Wilberforce believed, nonetheless, that England's destiny lay safest in the hands of men of clear Christian principle and that submission to Christ was a man's most important political as well as religious decision.[52]

> Accordingly, "very early in his own pilgrimage Wilberforce set out to bring his friends to Christ."[53] Wilberforce knew that salvation in and submission to Jesus Christ were preeminent factors in the life of effective politicians.[54]

Piper notes Wilberforce's strategy: "Alongside all his social engagements, he carried on a steady relational ministry, as we might call it, seeking to win his unbelieving colleagues to personal faith in Jesus Christ."[55]

Such a relationship with a fellow politician, Edward Eliot, serves to manifest the Christian/political philosophy of Wilberforce. Wilberforce won Eliot to Christ after the latter's wife died while giving birth. Subsequently, "The two [Wilberforce and Eliot] could open their hearts to each other. Both knew the difficulties of walking with God when pressed by the rush and other temptations of political life."[56]

Wilberforce's emphasis on evangelism throughout his political career remained consistent with his political philosophy. Conversely, present-day religious activists show little concern for the welfare of the heart of public servants. I know because I have witnessed this sad phenomenon for more than 25 years in ministry on capitol campuses. Rather, religious activists pressure those who know not the Author of Scripture to accede to the precepts of His book. I can tell you that little fruit results in that strategy.

Chapter 26

Wilberforce's Thoughts on Moralism

Wilberforce wrote a treatise in 1797 on the actual state of Christianity among the professing Christians of his day, titled *A Practical View of Christianity*.[57] Pollock notes, "*A Practical View* took the reader on a discursive journey to discover how Christianity should and could guide the politics, habits and attitudes of a nation from the highest to the lowest."[58]

In the treatise Wilberforce states that he wrote with the earnest intent "to point out the scanty and erroneous system of the bulk of those who belong to the class of orthodox Christians, and to contrast their defective scheme with a representation of what the author apprehends to be real Christianity."[59] The volume's depth proves especially remarkable considering Wilberforce regarded himself no more than a "layman."[60] Yet with doctrinal accuracy and prowess, Wilberforce outlined much of the failure of eighteenth-century British Christianity, exposing the deficiency he noted among so-called fellow Christians:

The truth is, their opinions on these subjects are not formed from the perusal of the Word of God. The Bible lies on the shelf unopened; and they would be wholly ignorant of its contents, except for what they hear occasionally at church, or for the faint traces which their memories may retain of the lessons of their earliest infancy.[61]

Wilberforce saw a deplorable lack of biblical reliance among the professing Theologically Liberal Christians of his day. [62] Sadly, such a state is far too often characteristic of the Church in the twenty-first century as well. Wilberforce drilled even deeper:

How different, nay, in many respects, how contradictory, would be the two systems of mere morals, of which the one should be formed from the commonly received maxims of the Christian world, and the other from the study of the holy Scriptures![63]

Wilberforce's distaste for rank moralism apart from a doctrinally rooted methodology of developing one's epistemology from the Word of God is readily apparent. To this statement Wilberforce adds the *coup de grâce* to any notion that he would support moralism in the public:

The diligent perusal of the Holy Scriptures would discover to us our past ignorance. We should cease to be deceived by superficial appearances, and to confound the Gospel of Christ with the systems of philosophers; we should become impressed with that weighty truth, so much forgotten, and never to be too strongly insisted on, that Christianity calls on us, as we value our immortal souls, not merely in general, to be religious and moral, but specially to believe the doctrines, and imbibe the principles, and practice the precepts of Christ.[64]

Accordingly,

> Wilberforce would not be pleased with those today who pin him up as the poster child for the moralistic Religious Right movement. Illustrating the point of this book, Wilberforce's emphasis on societal change was fueled by an evangelistic fervor.

His hopes were pinned on the truth of God's Word as the means of bringing solidarity to the nation and its people. For this reason, he held firm opinions about the role of the Church in promoting biblical understanding rather than moralistic campaigning. For example, in reaction to the radicals of his day, Wilberforce felt it necessary to...

> encourage the increase of devoted clergymen who would promote "true honest practical Christianity." He saw the role of clergy as that of reconcilers, harmonizers and quieters: he would not have liked radical parsons who preached political revolt, even against glaring injustice, for revolt bred distress and confusion for the common man. Wilberforce's eye was on the happiness of families rather than on the creation of a distant better order through civil strife; the French Revolution had been proof enough of the misery such might cause, and he was too near to appreciate its lasting contributions to liberty.[65]

SUMMARY

The ministry of evangelism and the discipleship of a governmental leader made William Wilberforce strong in Christ and subsequently broke the back of slavery in Britain.[66] And likewise, these objectives should be the primary ministry of the Church today.

Again, the institution of the Church should be pre-political rather than political. It should concentrate its energies on the primacy of evangelizing, teaching, and discipling public servants in Christ, rather than on becoming a political lobbying force on moral issues:[67] *leave that work to your disciples, for heaven's sake! That's their job and their calling—not yours!*

Pressure tactics may work effectively for a time, and they might even seem like the most practical way to achieve change in culture, yet Wilberforce "was practical with a difference. He believed with all his heart that new affections for God were the key to new morals and lasting political reformation."[68]

If Evangelicals in the political arena desire to have more Wilberforces in office—men and women whose most important political decision is their salvation and submission to God's Word—the biblical methodology to achieve this goal is only through the accurate proclamation of the truth of God's Word. Evangelism and discipleship of governmental leaders is the rightful and critically necessary place for the institutional Church within the halls of civil government.

John Piper sets forth the following challenge:

> Is it not remarkable that one of the greatest politicians of Britain and one of the most persevering public warriors for social justice should elevate doctrine so highly? Perhaps this is why the impact of the church today is as weak as it is. Those who are most passionate about being practical for the public good are often the least doctrinally interested or informed. Wilberforce would say: You can't endure in bearing fruit if you sever the root.[69]

How true this observation is and how sad as well. Wilberforce was not merely full of good and moral ideas; he was also full of God's wisdom and His Holy Spirit thanks to a humble pastor who evangelized and discipled him. As Romans 10:14 says, *How then will they call on Him in whom they have not believed? How will they believe in Him whom they have not heard? And how will they hear without a preacher?* This outcome illustrates the need for evangelizing and discipling today's governmental leaders! God may have dozens of Wilberforces in the making all around the world—maybe even two or three in our nation's Capitol!

Wilberforce serves as a pivotal Evangelical public servant role model! His story is an exemplar for every present and future public servant! States biographer Steven Gertz, who wrote about the life of Newton in "Pastor to the Nation":

> In 1786, Newton wrote of Wilberforce, "I hope the Lord will make him a blessing both as a Christian and a statesman. How seldom do these characters coincide! But they are not incompatible." To Newton's credit as a spiritual counselor and friend, few politicians have ever done so much as Wilberforce for the cause of Christ or the church.[70]

In many ways, William Wilberforce is a biblical role model of a most effective Evangelical public servant wherein the institutions of Church and State stay with their respective calling and, in so doing, achieve maximum impact!

The Church today needs more men like John Newton—men who will make disciples of Jesus Christ among those in political leadership. Making them disciples will enable them by the clear teaching of the Word of God to lead the State with visceral biblical convictions so as to achieve similar outcomes as Wilberforce—so as to turn *the world upside down*.

Are there Wilberforces in our time who are in the U.S. Congress, in the State Capitols, in the judges' chambers, in the school boards, in city halls and county governments across America and throughout the world, just waiting to be equipped, strengthened, and emboldened by the Word of God so they may fearlessly stand for His precepts? Are you the person who will reach them for Christ and, with them, be the next ones God chooses to turn *the world upside down*? Are you being called? If so, will you answer Him?

CONCLUSION

May we partner together to reach political leaders for Christ in America and throughout the world for the praise of Christ, the salvation of souls, the fulfillment of the Great Commission, and the preservation and illumination of our nation.

By this point, I hope you are asking, "How can I become involved in helping to reach political leaders for Christ?"

A movement for Christ among our nation's political leaders will occur only to the degree we establish strong, fruitful ministries in the federal and state capitols of our nation *and, in addition, in the thousands of local city and county government offices throughout our land.* This much larger portion of the initiative is perhaps where you can best play a key role in God's mission that can only be achieved by healthy, Bible-believing churches taking up the cause of founding and building (for starters) weekly Bible studies in these public buildings. (Keep in mind that the supposed legal prohibitions against using public buildings for Bible studies have been consistently defeated in the courts; usually only a sponsoring elected official is needed to host a Bible study in a government building.)

For example, your church might want to cater a weekly lunch at city hall or a county building or courthouse, and you could either help organize, host, or teach a Bible study for staff and elected and appointed officials. Capitol Ministries will provide more than 70 in-depth Bible studies that have been written specifically to meet the professional, personal, and faith needs of public servants.

I presently teach these studies and others to U.S. senators and representatives in Washington, D.C., and lead weekly studies remotely to former White House cabinet members and senior staff. A remote Bible study to America's governors has recently launched. Averaging eight pages long, the studies are published in the hardbound book *Oaks in Office: Essential Bible Studies for Political Leaders*, and they can be downloaded for free, chapter by chapter, from capmin.org. Each Bible study I write is exegetically deep, with specific applications to public servants.

Alternatively, you can download the same four-color Bible study that I am teaching that same week to our nation's leader in Washington, D.C., and follow along with us. These are only two of many ways believers can help reach political leaders for Christ. I am hereby issuing the call, and I hope we will soon see thousands of such ministries. Capitol Ministries is eager to train, mentor, help, serve, certify, equip, and provide ongoing support for the task!

By stepping out in faith in this manner, you will become acquainted with those in governmental leadership and therein establish a personal ministry, hopefully leading to their salvation and joining your local congregation! It is as simple as that to best impact our nation.

Capitol Ministries provides training, certification, and Bible study materials at no charge to help you build new ministries to local leaders in city and county governments. We also offer an annual national training conference for Local Government Ministry leaders. For more information, visit our website: capmin.org.

The body of Christ needs to found and maintain ministries to governmental leaders everywhere and at all levels of their career paths. By reigniting in our time the Bible's time-tested and successful top-down missions strategy to *all who are in authority*, together we can reach every elected official from the dogcatcher and librarian to the mayor and city and county officials throughout all of the state and federal governments of the world with the good news of new life in Christ! Where do you fit in?

ENDNOTES

PART I

1. *English Standard Version.*
2. In missiology, *people groups* generally means people of the same language.
3. In present-day missional understanding, an *affinity sphere* relates to a missions strategy of reaching people with a common vocation, whereas *a people group strategy* relates to reaching people with a common language.
4. William Penn, "Preface to the Frame of Government of the Colony of Pennsylvania, 1682," *The Founder's Constitution*, Vol. 1, Ch. 17, Doc. 4, 175–77. Retrieved from https://press-pubs.uchicago.edu/founders/documents/v1ch17s4.html.

PART II

1. *The Merriam-Webster Dictionary.* s.v. epoch, accessed June 1, 2021, https://www.merriam-webster.com/dictionary/epoch
2. Second Timothy 2:25 and other passages make it clear that both saving faith (see Ephesians 2:8–9) and repentance are gifts from God synonymously existing in and defining of God's gift of salvation in the life of an individual; it follows one cannot say "I have received Christ" without simultaneously declaring "I have repented of my sin."
3. *New American Standard Bible*: 1995 update. (Luke 3:3–14). LaHabra, Calif.: The Lockman Foundation, 1995. Used with permission.

    Four examples of parallel passages to Luke 3:3–14 and Ephesians 2 and 5—passages which similarly connect evangelism/ repentance with positive benefits to society in the here and now—are as follows (among many others):
    A. *"Wash yourselves, make yourselves clean; remove the evil of your deeds from My sight. Cease to do evil, learn to do good; seek justice, reprove the ruthless, defend the orphan, plead for the widow"* (Isaiah 1:16–18).
    B. *"But kept declaring both to those of Damascus first, and also at Jerusalem and then throughout all the region of Judea, and even to the Gentiles, that they should repent and turn to God, performing deeds appropriate to repentance"* (Acts 26:20).
    C. *But the fruit of the Spirit is love, joy, peace, patience, kindness, goodness, faithfulness, gentleness, self-control; against such things there is no law* (Galatians 5:22–23).
    D. *Having been filled with the fruit of righteousness which comes through Jesus Christ, to the glory and praise of God* (Philippians 1:11).

4. Leon Morris, *Tyndale New Testament Commentaries, the Gospel According to St. Luke* (Grand Rapids: Eerdmans, 1979), 96.
5. I. Howard Marshall, *The New International Greek Testament Commentary, The Gospel of Luke* (Grand Rapids: Eerdmans, 1978), 144.
6. "A soldier's remuneration was in fact low, and the temptation to increase it by rapacious dealings was strong." H. W. Heidland, *Theological Dictionary of the New Testament*, Vol. 5 (Grand Rapids: Eerdmans,1964–1976), 591f.
7. Note: I have referred to the Church now in a more specific manner: Evangelicalism. I am incorporating this change herein to define more narrowly what I mean as the Church. The Church as used to depict broader Protestantism (in the sense of Theological Liberalism), or Catholicism, or the Orthodox Church are not what I intend to include when I use the word "Church" in the context of this Bible study. I believe Evangelicalism is biblically representational more so of the biblical definition of "the Church" than the latter forms.
8. George M. Marsden, *Understanding Fundamentalism and Evangelicalism* (Grand Rapids: Eerdmans, 1991), 112.
9. See Bible study at capmin.org: "Better Understanding the Fallacy of Christian Nationalism."
10. Arthur Cushman McGiffert as quoted in G. Marsden, *Fundamentalism and American Culture: The Shaping of Twentieth-Century Evangelicalism* 1870–1925 (New York: Oxford University Press, 1980), 50.
11. For two of the best exegetical defenses of Premillennialism see: 1) Michael Vlach, *Premillennialism: Why There Must Be a Future Earthly Kingdom of Jesus* (Sun Valley, Calif.: Theological Studies Press, 2015) and 2) Matt Waymeyer, *Revelation 20 and the Millennial Debate* (Woodlands, Tex.; Kress Publications, 2004).
12. A theological discussion pertaining to the strengths and weaknesses of Postmillennialism warrants its own examination apart from this book.
13. See Brian Stanley, editor, *Christian Missions and the Enlightenment* (Nashville: Abingdon, Routledge Press, 2015). In this excellent series that traces world missions, it is evident that postmillennial eschatology as exported by missionaries did not work as a compelling force for evangelization of nations that were not inherently European/Christian based already. Postmillennial eschatology was not a tour de force for evangelistic endeavor because the objective of creating a Christian nation in a nation that is inherently otherwise is unrealistic. In an Islamic- or Hindu-based country (examples among many), a postmillennial eschatological motivation would make no sense as a means of compelling individual conversions.
14. J. Gresham Machen, *Christianity and Liberalism* (Grand Rapids: Eerdmans, 1923), 156.
15. "What is today a matter of academic speculation begins tomorrow to move armies and pull down empires." (J. Gresham Machen, *Christianity and Culture*, Princeton Theological Review 11 [1913], 7). The Religious Right movement emphasized policy change to such a heightened degree that evangelism of souls in the capital community was eclipsed.
16. George Marsden, *Fundamentalism and American Culture: The Shaping of the Twentieth Century* (New York: Oxford Press, Inc., 2006), 18.
17. Stanley Gundry, *Love Them in: The Life and Theology of D. L. Moody* (Chicago: Northfield Publishers, 1999).
18. Ibid.
19. Joel A. Carpenter, *Revive Us Again: The Reawakening of American Fundamentalism* (New York: Oxford University Press, 1997), 36.
20. Ibid., 11.
21. Machen, *Christianity and Liberalism*.

22. Ned B. Stonehouse, *J. Gresham Machen, A Biographical Memoir* (Grand Rapids: Eerdmans, 1955).
23. Many of the elected leaders with whom I counsel experience this ostracism, in our understanding of this matter.
24. *Christian Life Magazine*, Vol. 17 No. 11, March 1956.
25. Ibid.
26. Ibid.
27. See *The Lausanne Covenant*, The Lausanne Committee on World Evangelization at www.lausanne.org. One of the takeaways of this historic gathering was the ensuing statement from the convention that the Church needed to possess "two wings on the bird" so to speak. By that idiom they meant one of evangelism and the other of social involvement. The inclusion of this represents perhaps the Neo-evangelical influence present at the convention. The famous British theologian, John Stott, was to write the theology for the second aspect of this statement to justify its inclusion, but it never materialized beyond a simple listing of scriptural references in supposed support of the previously written summary statement. The wording and organizational outline in the Lausanne Covenant appears to give equal weight to evangelism and social involvement. But these two directives are not biblically on equal ground. Based on Scripture, this is faulty theology. The Bible teaches (cf. Matthew 5:16) *that social involvement is a means to an end—to be used by the Christian to achieve the ultimate objective of evangelism*. Spiritual maturation (Matthew 5:1–12) leads to cultural participation (Matthew 5:13–15), which ultimately leads to the evangelization of others (Matthew 5:16). Personal spiritual maturation will be indicated by one's cultural participation, which then testifies of God and one's need for Him in a fallen, onlooking world. This progression reveals the biblical formula for being an effective ambassador for Christ.
28. Jerry Falwell, *Falwell: An Autobiography* (Lynchburg: Liberty House Publishers, 1997).
29. Tom Minnery, *Why You Can't Stay Silent: A Biblical Mandate to Shape Our Culture* (Wheaton: Tyndale House Publishers, 2001).

PART III

1. I have visited many democratically governed nations where righteousness does not exist to the degree it should, and it is easy to see how the nation is hindered as a result.
2. From the preface to the Charter of Liberties and Frame of Government of Pennsylvania, 1682; *Colonial Origins of the American Constitution: A Documentary History*, ed. Donald S. Lutz (Indianapolis: Liberty Fund, 1998).
3. See Leonard Verduin, *The Reformers and Their Stepchildren* (Grand Rapids, Eerdmans, 1964).
4. Charles Bridges, *A Commentary on Proverbs* (New York/Pittsburgh: R. Carter, 1847).
5. For more than 70 in-depth Bible studies to political leaders see *Oaks in Office: Essential Bible Studies for Political Leaders* by Ralph Drollinger.

PART IV

1. The Bible student will note that oftentimes a NT principle, stated in a tight fashion, is illustrated by a long narrative passage in the OT. Such is the case here: Hebrews 12:5–11 is illustrated in and by the events recorded in Haggai chapter 1. This correlation speaks to the analogy of Scripture—written by God via different authors at different times. The reader will note later the same with Matthew 6:33.

2. After the death of King Solomon (sometime around 930 BC), God's kingdom of Israel split into a northern kingdom, which retained the name Israel (also called Ephraim) and a southern kingdom called Judah. Judah and Ephraim both got their names after the tribe of Judah and the tribe of Ephraim respectively, two of the twelve tribes of Israel that dominated those kingdoms. Both kingdoms would go into exile. The book of Haggai provides a spiritual insight into the kingdom of Judah right after Judah had returned from the Babylonian/Persian captivity.
3. In his commentary on Zephaniah and Haggai, J. Vernon McGee is careful to include the parallel passage found in Ezra 3:8–13. Therein is revealed the fact that the older remnant who had seen Solomon's Temple before their exile and had returned to the Promised Land were complaining by making comparison. See J. Vernon McGee, *Zephaniah and Haggai* (La Verne, Calif.: El Camino Press, 1979), 82–86.
4. There are 12 second-person plural pronouns—*you*—that follow 1:1 prior to 1:12. It follows that all of them directly and only apply to Zerubbabel and Joshua. It is not until verse 12 that Haggai includes "all the remnant of the people" and states thereinafter "their God" utilizing third person pronouns. In fact, many of the 12 "yous" are supplied in the NASB English translation of the original Hebrew text for the sake of readability, but the point still stands that only two individuals are initially held responsible for Judah's possible judgment by God (yet again!).
5. This passage serves to reveal that God continues to abide by—and expects His postexilic chosen people to continue to abide by—the "if/then" promise of the Abrahamic Covenant as recorded in Deuteronomy 28.
6. The Temple represents God's dwelling place and symbolizes His manifest presence with His chosen people. It carries with it the idea of God's dwelling glory with His people (cf. Ezekiel 8–11). Accordingly, Haggai's addressing the people's laxness in rebuilding His Temple carries the idea of the existence of an overall spiritual lethargy—if not rejection of God in their lives.
7. Cf: Robert B. Chisholm, Jr., *Interpreting the Minor Prophets* (Grand Rapids, Academic Books, Zondervan Publishers, 1989), 221.
8. Not long after this, a study of the book of Ezra reveals Judah backslid again. When Ezra arrived with the second wave of returnees from their prior captivity, Ezra revives them once again by teaching the Word of God.
9. The dual address of Haggai's rebuke in 1:1 is not forgotten here. In Haggai 1:1, the prophet is rebuking both the civil leader, Zerubbabel, and the spiritual leader, Joshua. Our nation today (in addition to the obedience of our civil leaders who name the name of Christ) is also in dire need of our spiritual leaders, i.e., church pastors walking in obedience to God's purposes. The primary responsibility of today's pastors is teaching the whole counsel of God to their congregations (cf. Hosea 4:6; Acts 20:27–28) and making disciples (Matthew 28:18–20). Most churches today do not follow those directives, and it stands to reason that our nation suffers as a result. There are many reasons why the American Church is impotent today as compared to the first-century Church, which **turned the world upside down** (cf. Acts 17:6).

First, Theologically Liberal churches do not preach a salvific gospel; rather, they teach a "Social Gospel," which is not biblical and does not lead to individual salvation nor the filling and empowering of the Holy Spirit in the life of the believer. Additionally, many Evangelical churches are "seeker" driven, meaning they teach watered-down, feel-good messages to keep the unsaved coming back without ever teaching them the whole counsel of God (Acts 20:27). Lastly, hyper-charismatic and prosperity church movements are, at their core, experiential and self-interest oriented. Few churches today are biblical and committed to teaching the "whole purpose of God" (Acts 20:27). All those aberrant forms of Christianity stand in juxtaposition to expository, exegetical regular instruction from the spiritual leader. Biblically driven churches explain mankind's need for Jesus as Savior, feed the saints a high-protein diet of the unedited Word of God, build spiritual musculature, and mature believers: they "make disciples," per the command in Matthew 28:19–20. At the end of the day, the vast majority of "churches" today that are Theological Liberal, watered-down, experiential and/or self-interest oriented do not create strong ambassadors for Christ who impact the direction of our nation. Haggai would rebuke all of those aberrant spiritual leaders today.

10. In my Bible study, "Does God Judge Nations Today?" I build the case exegetically and theologically that God does not judge nations today in terms of cataclysmic or abandonment forms of His wrath. But I do state that sowing-and-reaping wrath is prevalent in all epochs of biblical history—in terms of individuals, groups of individuals, and nations as a whole. Accordingly, in that Haggai 1 is illustrative of the manifestation of sowing-and-reaping wrath, the principle can be appropriately applied in the Church Age. If political and spiritual leaders sow spiritual lethargy in any age and time, it stands to reason that the nation is subject to reaping God's respective wrath.

I think of the principle of Haggai in this way: what a leader sows a nation reaps. That was true with returning Judah and remains true in any nation today. Summarily, this axiom begs for the church to disciple political leaders!

PART V

1. "Britain and the Slave Trade," The National Archives, Retrieved from https://www.nationalarchives.gov.uk/education/resources/abolition-slavery/.
2. For more on this topic see: H. Shelton Smith, Robert T. Handy, and Lefferts A. Loetscher, *American Christianity: An Historical Interpretation with Representative Documents*, Vol. 2, 1820–1960 (New York: Charles Scribner's Sons, 1963), 167–212.
3. George M. Marsden, *Religion and American Culture*, 2nd ed. (Fort Worth, Tex.: Harcourt College Publishers, 2001), 74.
4. That which germinated the overturn of slavery in America was not political activism, Abraham Lincoln, or the Civil War. It was the winning out of correct Bible interpretation, and that correct theology influenced the State. By way of application, that is why Bible study among public servants is so astronomically important—because politics and policy, wars and actions stem from the beliefs people hold close in their hearts. Actions are reflective, whereas beliefs are causal.
5. To get a sense of the political courage necessary to lead this charge, consider the following: "Britain two hundred years ago was the world's leading slave-trading nation; uprooting the vile practice threatened the annual trade of hundreds of ships, thousands of sailors, and hundreds of millions of pounds sterling." [John Pollock, "A Man Who Changed His Times," in *Character Counts: Leadership Qualities in Washington, Wilberforce, Lincoln, and Solzhenitsyn*, ed. by Os Guinness (Grand Rapids: Baker Book House, 1999), 81.]
6. It is generally accepted that the goal of the Christian political activist movement in America is to increase societal morality. The method employed by this movement to reach this goal is political in nature, i.e., the passage and enforcement of laws that promote morality.

7. One of many examples is The Wilberforce Forum, which is a subsidiary of Prison Fellowship. The Annual Wilberforce Forum Award "recognizes an individual who has made a difference in the face of formidable societal problems and injustices." https://en-academic.com/dic.nsf/enwiki/750544.
8. This same God-given wisdom is available to every Christian legislator today who believes in Jesus Christ and submits himself/herself to the Word of God.
9. William Wilberforce, *A Practical View of Christianity*, ed. Kevin Charles Belmonte, with an introduction by Charles Colson (Peabody, Mass.: Hendrickson Publishers, Inc., 1996), 5–6. Respected author and Bible teacher John Piper wisely suggests, "To understand and appreciate the life and labor of William Wilberforce, one of the wisest things to do is to read his own book, *A Practical View of Christianity*, first, and then read biographies" [John Piper, *The Roots of Endurance: Invincible Perseverance in the Lives of John Newton, Charles Simeon, and William Wilberforce* (Wheaton, Ill.: Crossway Books, 2002), 117]. Let the reader also read Piper's book, *The Roots of Endurance* for a cogent synthesis on the vibrant faith in Christ that fueled Wilberforce's political efforts. The politician who is willing to study the life of William Wilberforce through his writings and those writings about him will be richer for the experience.
10. Though Wilberforce was personally encouraged by both Wesley and Newton, "almost certainly he never heard Whitefield, who in the early autumn of 1769, at about the time of William's coming south, left for his sixth and last visit to America, where he died." [John Pollock, *Wilberforce* (New York: St. Martin's Press, 1977), 5.
11. Contra, Charles Colson, introduction to *A Practical View of Christianity*, William Wilberforce, xxii (Peabody, Mass.: Hendrickson Publishers, Inc., 2006). Colson writes, "By the time Wilberforce knew of him, Newton was a clergyman in the Church of England, renowned for his outspokenness on spiritual matters."
12. Pollock, *Wilberforce*, 4.
13. Pollock, "A Man Who Changed His Times," 79.
14. Steven Gertz, "Pastor to the Nation" in *Christian History & Biography*, Issue 81, Winter 2004, 37. "Newton responded to thousands of requests for spiritual counsel with letters advising the lowly and the great."
15. Pollock, *Wilberforce*, 5.
16. Piper, 123.
17. Ibid.
18. Pollock, *Wilberforce*, 6.
19. Piper, 123.
20. Pollock, "A Man Who Changed His Times," 79.
21. Pollock, *Wilberforce*, 33. Pollock further states of Wilberforce's spiritual instruction at that time: "In no sense was he an atheist. Lindsey's disciples at Essex Street worshipped the Deity, a benevolent Providence in some way also the judge of man's actions, but they rejected Christ's divinity, the Christian view of the Atonement, and the authority of Scripture." (Pollock, *Wilberforce*, 33–34). Wilberforce may have been no atheist, yet neither was he a Bible-believing Christian!
22. Pollock, *Wilberforce*, 35.
23. J. Douglas Holladay, "A Life of Significance," in *Character Counts: Leadership Qualities in Washington, Wilberforce, Lincoln, and Solzhenitsyn*, ed. by Os Guinness (Grand Rapids, Mich.: Baker Book House, 1999).

24. Charles Colson, "Introduction," xxi. Pollock writes of the situation: "Wilberforce was looking for a traveling companion. He 'had no one else in mind when the family went to Scarborough, Yorkshire's fashionable watering place, for the summer season. Here he fell in with the huge Isaac Milner, his former usher at Hull Grammar School who now was a tutor of Queen's College, Cambridge. On impulse, apparently, Wilberforce invited Milner, all expenses paid.'" (Pollock, *Wilberforce*, 32).

Notes Pollack of Wilberforce's and Milner's initial acquaintance, "Isaac [Milner] would one day influence William Wilberforce profoundly, but their paths crossed only briefly at Hull Grammar School." (Pollock, *Wilberforce*, 4).

25. Pollock, *Wilberforce*, 35.
26. Ibid., 36.
27. Ibid., 37.
28. Colson, "*Introduction*," xxi.
29. Ibid.
30. Pollock, *Wilberforce*, 38.
31. Gertz, 37.
32. Pollock, *Wilberforce*, 44.
33. Ibid., 44.
34. Ibid., 146.
35. Ibid., 46.
36. Holladay, 69.
37. Garth Lean, *God's Politician: William Wilberforce's Struggle* (Colorado Springs, Colo.: Helmers & Howard, 1987), 3.
38. Holladay, 69.
39. "Of course the opposition that raged for these twenty years [of Wilberforce's legislative battle] was because of the financial benefits of slavery to the traders and to the British economy, because of what the plantations in the West Indies produced" (Piper, 130–31).
40. Charles Colson, "Introduction," in *Wilberforce, A Practical View of Christianity*, xxii.
41. John Pollock, "A Man Who Changed His Times," 86.
42. Explains Piper, "By that term [peculiar doctrines], he simply meant the central distinguishing doctrines of human depravity, divine judgment, the substitutionary work of Christ on the cross, justification by faith alone, regeneration by the Holy Spirit, and the practical necessity of fruit in a life devoted to good deeds" (Piper, 120).
43. Piper, 118.
44. William Wilberforce cited in Piper, 116.
45. Pollock, "A Man Who Changed His Times," 87.
46. While there is no biblical mandate to shape our culture (as is the subtitle of one popular Religious Right book), there is a biblical formula as expressed herein as to how one best shapes culture.
47. Holladay, 70.
48. Piper, 117.
49. It is noteworthy to add here that Wilberforce was a man of prayer. Writes E. M. Bounds: Said William Wilberforce, the peer of kings: "I must secure more time for private devotions. I have been living far too public for me. The shortening of private devotions starves the soul; it grows lean and faint. I have been keeping too late hours." Of a failure in Parliament he says: "Let me record my grief and shame, and all, probably, from private devotions having been contracted, and so God let me stumble." More solitude and earlier hours were his

remedy. [Edward M. Bounds, *Power Through Prayer*, (Oak Harbor, Wash.: Logos Research Systems, Inc., 1999), Retrieved from https://www.leaderu.com/cyber/books/bounds/powc15-20.html, chapter 19.]

This resolve shows maturity in Wilberforce's Christian life and suggests that even his political endeavors were bathed in prayer and supplication before God. Note also Wilberforce's opening quotation in the same chapter of Bounds' book:

> This perpetual hurry of business and company ruins me in soul if not in body. More solitude and earlier hours! I suspect I have been allotting habitually too little time to religious exercises, as private devotion and religious meditation, Scripture-reading, etc. Hence I am lean and cold and hard. I had better allot two hours or an hour and a half daily. I have been keeping too late hours, and hence have had but a hurried half hour in a morning to myself. Surely the experience of all good men confirms the proposition that without a due measure of private devotions the soul will grow lean. But all may be done through prayer—almighty prayer, I am ready to say—and why not? For that it is almighty is only through the gracious ordination of the God of love and truth. O then, pray, pray, pray! [E. M. Bounds, *Power Through Prayer*.]

50. Piper, 128; as quoting from Robert Isaac Wilberforce and Samuel Wilberforce, *The Life of William Wilberforce*, abridged edition (London, 1843), 47.
51. The mature believer can see through his temptation with the biblical discernment of Ephesians 6:12: ***For our struggle is not against flesh and blood, but against the rulers, against the powers, against the world forces of this darkness, against the spiritual forces of wickedness in the heavenly places.***
52. Pollock, *Wilberforce*, 66.
53. Ibid. This is congruous with a clear biblical understanding and all that Wilberforce has already reasoned. However, his use of ecumenical tactics to achieve greater power, influence, and reelection do not meet the test of Scripture. Holladay outlines Wilberforce's philosophy in seven principles.
54. After all, Romans 13:4 calls elected political leaders ***ministers of God for good***.
55. Piper, 134. In his book, Pollock pays tribute to Wilberforce's Christian influence among his colleagues when he writes, "In contrast to 1780, when scarcely one man of strong religious and humanitarian conviction sat in the House of Commons, Wilberforce had many disciples." (Pollock, *Wilberforce*, 279.)
56. Pollock, *Wilberforce*, 66. Pollock notes God's salvific work in Eliot's life. For instance, "Wilberforce's sympathy became one of Eliot's chief props in the months that followed [after his wife died giving birth], until he grew to share Wilberforce's faith. 'I was little better than an infidel,' Eliot commented some years later, 'but it pleased God to draw me by [the bereavement] to a better mind.'" [Pollock, *Wilberforce*, 65.]
57. According to Pollock, "*A Practical View* is a Biblical view, presented intelligibly if haphazardly. It sets out the essential Christian doctrines by Scripture texts, and then discourses about the imitation which passed for religion in 1797. The very discursiveness which powered the book's impact on a generation rather bored by closely reasoned theologies, makes it wearisome to the modern reader and checkmates literary and theological critiques: it is a slippery eel of a book." [Pollock, *Wilberforce*, 147].
58. Pollock, *Wilberforce*, 148.
59. Wilberforce, *A Practical View of Christianity*, xxxi.
60. Ibid., xxx.
61. Ibid., 4.

62. "The more he [Wilberforce] looked at the religion of the New Testament, the more he wanted to show how far it lay from the religion of the polite in England, whose blend of a little piety with a little moralizing offered nothing to a man whose inward eye had seen his corruption in the blinding light of the glory of the Lord." [Pollock, *Wilberforce*, 146].
63. Wilberforce, *A Practical View of Christianity*, 4.
64. Ibid, 5-6.
65. Pollock, *Wilberforce*, 259.
66. His personal pursuit of growing in Christ (i.e., studying the Word, praying diligently, valuing doctrine over moralism, etc.) kept Wilberforce strong.
67. This statement is not to be confused with every believer's responsibility as a citizen to vote. I am talking about mobilizing the institution of the Church into a lobbying organization at the expense of its calling to make disciples.
68. Piper, 119.
69. Ibid., 159–60.
70. Steven Gertz, "Pastor to the Nation," 39.

ABOUT THE AUTHOR

Ralph Drollinger, President and Founder of Capitol Ministries, leads separate Bible studies every week on the Hill in Washington, D.C., to U.S. senators and representatives. He also leads a Bible study remotely via the internet for America's sitting and former governors and former White House cabinet members and senior staff.

Capitol Ministries was founded by Ralph and Danielle Drollinger in 1996 with the mission of making disciples of Jesus Christ in the political arena throughout the world. To date, the ministry has established discipleship Bible-study ministries to legislators in 43 states, to city and county local leaders in communities in nine states. Ministries have also been launched to local, regional, and national political leaders and parliamentarians in 43 foreign nations.

Ralph is an expository historical evangelical pastor who teaches the Bible one book at a time, verse by verse. Additionally, every week Bible studies that Ralph has written on topical issues are delivered to several hundred U.S. senators and representatives and are sent via email to thousands of people who request them. Ralph believes that nothing can substitute this basic discipline in ministry. Transformation and discipleship stem from *the renewing of your mind* (Romans 12:1–2).

Ralph earned a Bachelor of Arts degree in Geography/Ecosystems from the University of California, Los Angeles (UCLA). He earned a Master of Divinity degree from The Master's Seminary.

He played basketball at UCLA under coach John Wooden and was the first player in NCAA history to go to four Final Four tournaments. Ralph was taken in the NBA Draft three times but chose to forgo the NBA to instead play with Athletes in Action, an evangelistic basketball team that toured the world and preached the gospel at halftimes. In June 1980, Ralph signed with the Dallas Mavericks as a free agent, becoming the first Dallas Maverick in the history of the then-new NBA franchise.

A former world-class mountaineer, Ralph is the first person to have climbed every peak on the main ridge of the Sierra Nevada between Olancha and Sonora Pass, CA, the 250 mile section known as the High Sierra. Ralph and Danielle have three married children and seven grandchildren.

Ralph is also the author of *Rebuilding America: The Biblical Blueprint* and *Oaks in Office: Essential Bible Studies for Political Leaders*.

Also available
FROM RALPH DROLLINGER

Oaks in Office
Essential Bible Studies for Political Leaders

This multi-volume book set contains in-depth and comprehensive Bible studies that have been written to meet the political leader's spiritual needs—both personal and professional.

The Bible studies were written to lead the political leader to Christ, teach him the Word of God, and disciple him to maturity in the Faith. Delving deeply into Scripture, political leaders may develop in personal holiness, establish a biblical foundation, come to comprehend, and form a biblical worldview, and increase in faith and personal courage.

The title *Oaks in Office* was inspired by the oak tree which becomes the mighty oak by sending a taproot deep into the earth to find a dependable source of moisture and nutrition. From this depth, it grows an elaborate root system that spreads up to seven times the width of its leafy crown. These sturdy and durable roots will bring the tree moisture and sustenance all its life. So, too, will the Word of God nurture the faithful Christian public servant throughout his life.

Ralph asks, "How can we expect someone who rejects the author of Scripture to accept the precepts of His book?"

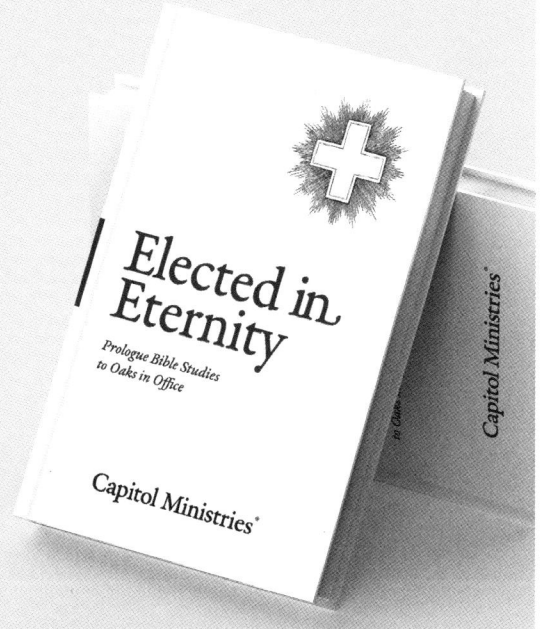

Also available
FROM CAPITOL MINISTRIES

Elected in Eternity
Prologue Bible Studies to Oaks in Office

The Bible studies in *Elected in Eternity* offer an introduction to the Christian faith and serve as a vital complement to the studies in *Oaks in Office*.

Elected in Eternity covers basic Christian tenets. Bible studies in the book introduce the seeker, the new believer, or the seasoned Christian who desires to learn more, an intimate introduction to Christ, His attributes, gifts, purpose, roles, and His sacrificial gift to mankind as Lord and Savior. The studies also inform the believer of his obligations to God, reveal the responses God expects from believers to His directives, and discloses the relationship God desires to have with each believer and how that is achieved.

Provided in a workbook format, *Elected in Eternity* offers the reader the opportunity to take notes that will benefit him when he delves into the deeper studies in *Oaks in Office*. Without this rudimentary understanding of the basics of Christianity, the student of *Oaks in Office* may become overwhelmed. It is recommended that both books be studied in a small group.